LEARNING AGILITY

LEARNING AGILITY

The Key to Leader Potential

2nd Edition

David F Hoff and W. Warner Burke

For information, contact Hogan Press
11 S. Greenwood, Tulsa OK 74120
hoganassessments.com

ISBN: 979-8-9856452-6-2

Interior Book Design by
Michelle M. White Graphic Design

HOGANPRESS

This edition is dedicated to
my wife Susan, who supported my passion for learning globally
which we now pursue together.

Thanks to Silse Martell for her fresh ideas and
other contributions to this edition.

CONTENTS

PROLOGUE   1

SECTION I

CHAPTER 1
What is Learning Agility—and Why Now?   7

CHAPTER 2
Learning Agility: A Summary of Theory   17

CHAPTER 3
How to Measure Learning Agility: Developing the
Burke Learning Agility Assessment   29

CHAPTER 4
Interpreting the *Burke Learning Agility
Self-Assessment Report*   35

SECTION II

CHAPTER 5
Flexibility   77

CHAPTER 6
Speed   85

CHAPTER 7
Experimenting   91

CHAPTER 8
Performance Risk Taking   99

CHAPTER 9
Interpersonal Risk Taking   107

CHAPTER 10
Collaborating 115

CHAPTER 11
Information Gathering 123

CHAPTER 12
Feedback Seeking 131

CHAPTER 13
Reflecting 139

SECTION III

CHAPTER 14
Integrating the *Burke Learning Agility Self-Assessment
Report* into Training, Orientation and Induction Programs 149

CHAPTER 15
Integrating the *Burke Learning Agility Self-Assessment
Report* into Individual Assessments 155

CHAPTER 16
Integrating the *Burke Learning Agility Inventory
Self-Assessment Report* into Performance Management
and Development 163

CHAPTER 17
Integrating the *Burke Learning Agility Self-Assessment
Report* into Succession Planning 173

CHAPTER 18
Integrating the *Burke Learning Agility Self-Assessment
Report* with Coaching 183

CHAPTER 19
Using the *Burke Learning Agility Inventory Self-Assessment
Report* as an Organizational Development Intervention 189

EPILOGUE 217

REFERENCES 219

PROLOGUE

Since the first edition of this book, the world hasn't just changed—it's been jolted, fractured, and fast-forwarded. We lived through a global pandemic, watched power dynamics shift across continents, and braced as trade wars rocked economies.

Then came Artificial Intelligence—fuel to a fire already burning fast—shattering every notion of what "rapid transformation" means. In this chaos, one truth stands firm: organizations rise or fall on the strength of their people. The real question—the million-dollar question—is this: **what does it take to lead when the world won't stop moving?**

The answer to this question, more than ever before, is Learning Agility—the flexible and rapid way of learning and applying new skills and knowledge needed for organizations to thrive in complex, uncertain, and accelerated business environments.

While the concept of learning agility isn't new, only recently has research proven it can be measured reliably at the individual level, thanks to the work of Emeritus Columbia University Professor Warner Burke. That breakthrough led to the development of the Burke Learning Agility Inventory—the first theory-based assessment designed to quantify learning agility and offer meaningful developmental insights.

This book is your guide to understanding, measuring, and applying learning agility in practical, high-impact ways.

WHAT'S INSIDE

This introduction will walk you through what to expect in the chapters ahead.

- **Chapter 1 makes the case for why learning agility matters now more than ever—and why it's critical to talk about it today.**

- Chapters 2 through 4 lay out the theory behind learning agility and explain how that theory led to the creation and validation of the Burke Learning Agility Inventory, Dr. W. Warner Burke identified nine key dimensions that make up learning agility. Each dimension has a one-line definition, and if a person is demonstrating the behaviors described, they're showing that capability—though capability can vary in strength and complexity.

Chapter 4 also includes a sample assessment report, complete with interpretation tips and guidance on how to build strength in each area.

SECTION II: BUILDING AGILITY IN INDIVIDUALS

Chapters 5 through 13 dive into each of the nine learning agility dimensions—one chapter per dimension. Each chapter follows a consistent structure:

- A snapshot of what the dimension looks like in real life.
- A simple, one-sentence definition.
- A story or literary excerpt that vividly illustrates the dimension in action.
- Examples of how the dimension appears at different levels in the workplace—from individual contributors to managers to senior leaders.

We also feature practical development scenarios, based on assessment results, where individuals grow a specific capability through on-the-job assignments, projects, or coaching. For many line managers, this section may be the most immediately actionable—and a natural place to pause before diving deeper.

SECTION III: LEARNING AGILITY ACROSS THE TALENT LIFECYCLE

The final seven chapters (14–19) focus on applying learning agility in real-world organizational contexts. While designed with HR and L&D

professionals in mind, these insights are valuable for any leader responsible for talent decisions.

- Chapter 14 explores how to use the self-assessment in training programs. Every training effort is a learning opportunity—and orientation is the perfect moment to start a conversation about agility strengths and development needs.
- Chapter 15 examines learning agility in assessment and selection. While more research is needed to fully link agility with personality traits, early findings suggest promising insights for identifying potential.
- Chapter 16 focuses on performance and development. Some companies have abandoned performance management systems—but we believe the conversation should evolve, not end. Learning agility gives managers better tools to talk about growth and guide development.
- Chapter 17 adds learning agility to the succession planning conversation. If potential is about navigating new, complex challenges and figuring things out on the fly—then learning agility is at its core.
- Chapter 18 is about coaching. Whether internal or external, coaching is more impactful when grounded in a person's learning agility profile. It helps both coach and coachee zero in on what really matters.
- Chapter 19 zooms out to the team and organizational level. How can leaders use this assessment with their teams? How can departments or even entire organizations embed learning agility into their culture? We're just beginning to explore these frontiers—and the potential is enormous.

In the spirit of learning, growing, and adapting, we invite you to read on—and then share your experiences with us. Because if there's one thing we know for sure, it's this: the future belongs to the agile.

SECTION I

CHAPTER 1

WHAT IS LEARNING AGILITY—AND WHY NOW?

Learning agility is quickly emerging as one of the most critical skills for leadership—and it's not just a passing trend. It's here to stay. At its core, learning agility is the ability to navigate new experiences, experiment with new behaviors, seek feedback, and adapt quickly—especially when the path isn't clear. It's about learning *in real time* and turning every challenge, even unfamiliar ones, into a stepping stone for growth.

Learning agility is a game-changer at every level. For executives, it fuels more dynamic, forward-thinking leadership. For mid-level managers, it offers a roadmap to accelerate growth and overcome hidden barriers. For teams, it builds stronger collaboration, adaptability, and performance. And for anyone looking to stretch, evolve, and thrive professionally, learning agility unlocks potential in a way few other skills can.

Most importantly, learning agility is now a cornerstone of **future readiness**—the ability for individuals, teams, and entire organizations to transform quickly and thrive, whether they see change coming or are blindsided by it. Future readiness is no longer a "nice to have"; it's mission-critical. It's showing up in corporate strategy sessions, leadership development programs, and even global indexes from organizations like the World Economic Forum and IMD.

In a world defined by constant disruption, rising expectations, and deep uncertainty, there has never been a more urgent time to embrace learning agility.

For years, defining, measuring, and applying learning agility felt like chasing something just out of reach. But today, the curtain has been pulled back. What once seemed elusive is now clear—and it's more essential and transformative than ever before.

THE CASE FOR LEARNING AGILITY

Let me give you a personal example.

For years, I worked at a company many would describe as great—particularly by financial standards. On paper, it was a success story. But that success became a trap. It bred complacency at the top. Confident in their track record, senior leaders were slow to adapt, resistant to feedback, and lacked the urgency to evolve.

This was a Fortune 100 company, poised for international expansion. But the strategies that had propelled its U.S. success didn't translate overseas. What worked at home fell flat abroad. While the world changed around it, the company failed to adjust.

It was a good company, maybe even a great one. But in order to sustain its success and continue growing, it needed to expand into international markets. Growth, after all, is one of the clearest markers of long-term success.

Yet the very frameworks and perspectives that had fueled its achievements in the U.S. proved ineffective—and even irrelevant—abroad. The company failed to adapt to the vastly different contexts it encountered. Ultimately, it was acquired by a non-U.S. competitor that was able to quickly understand the landscape, reframe its approach, and act decisively.

They weren't alone. Back then, the business world lionized financial performance as the gold standard. Books like *Good to Great* by Jim Collins were cited like scripture. Collins famously wrote, *"Good is the enemy of great,"* and defined greatness in terms of shareholder value. Companies were admired for their balance sheets, not their ability to learn, adapt, or grow.

But over time, many of Collins's "great" companies stumbled. The traits he identified didn't guarantee future success. The rearview mirror doesn't predict the road ahead.

In the 1980s, two major business movements—**business process reengineering** and **continuous improvement**—captured the imagination of leaders around the world. These efforts promised significant savings and, in many cases, delivered real, measurable results. But in my former company, some of these initiatives were eventually abandoned. Why? Because they demanded deep, foundational changes. They were too difficult to implement. The cost of change simply exceeded the perceived payoff.

And yet, the pace of change has only accelerated. Today, organizations must navigate a relentless mix of **political, economic, social, and technological** disruptions. Like whitewater rapids, these forces come at us fast and without warning.

The only constant is our capacity to **recognize or anticipate change** and to **adapt our mindset and approach accordingly.** That's what learning agility empowers us to do: to keep moving with the current, rather than against it.

Once we detect that something in our environment has shifted, learning agility enables us to respond. We can **experiment, seek feedback, gather new information, collaborate, take risks, and reflect**—not just on our performance, but on what we're learning along the way.

There's another reason the time for learning agility is now: **the U.S. workforce is undergoing a profound transformation.**

Baby Boomers—those born between 1946 and 1961—are now at or beyond retirement age. This generation, 76 million strong, has essentially phased out of the workforce.

In their place, are **Millennials**—born between 1977 and 2004. Numbering over 71 million, they are now filling the pipeline of leadership. Unlike Boomers, Millennials tend to be driven more by opportunities to learn and grow, and less by loyalty to a specific organization. To retain top talent in this generation, companies need to keep them engaged. One powerful way to do this is by giving them opportunities to **use and stretch their learning agility**—or to develop it where it may be lacking.

Enter **Gen Z**—the next emerging generation. They are digital natives who've grown up with technology in every aspect of life. They are the most racially and ethnically diverse generation yet, and they carry a new set of expectations. They're not looking to fight for diversity, equity, and inclusion—they expect it. For them, a diversity of voices and perspectives isn't a "nice to have"—it's the starting point. And learning agility? They'll see it not as an optional skill, but as an essential capability to develop and leverage in every role.

That truth came crashing down where I worked. Though the company looked strong, it lacked agility. Its leaders couldn't shift quickly enough to meet change. At the time, even if we had identified learning agility as the missing piece, we had no way to measure or nurture it.

Now, nearly 20 years later, we can.

We finally have tools that help us recognize who the agile learners are—the ones who can learn what they need today to succeed tomorrow. And that changes everything.

CRACKING THE CODE

For years, researchers, professors, and leadership experts have tried to predict leadership potential. The answer, in large part, has been right in front of us: learning agility.

The challenge wasn't in recognizing its importance—it was in measuring it.

That's where Emeritus Columbia University Professor Warner Burke comes in. He saw both the promise and the problem. With students at Teachers College, Columbia University he developed the 38 items used to measure learning agility. These items were then tested for psychometric structure and reliability in concert with the Center for Creative Leadership. Possessing the validated items Burke began a collaboration with EASI Consult Principals David Hoff and David Smith to put the items on their testing platform and create a report describing a person's level of learning agility. This resulted in the Burke Learning Agility Inventory™—the first validated tool for measuring learning agility.

Burke's work to understand what agile learners have in common, led to a simple but powerful definition:

> *"Learning agility is dealing with new experiences flexibly*
> *and rapidly by trying new behavior, getting feedback on*
> *these attempts, and making quick adjustments so new learning*
> *will be realized when you do not know exactly what to do."*
> *—Burke, 2016*

The definition may be straightforward, but building a tool to reliably measure its dimensions took years of rigorous research.

That work laid the foundation for Burke Learning Agility Inventory™—which I now have the privilege to carry forward as part of Burke Assessments.

The nine dimensions of learning agility as defined by Burke and their associated definitions are as follows:

- *Flexibility* – Being open to new ideas and proposing new solutions.
- *Speed* – Acting on ideas quickly so that those that aren't working are discarded and other possibilities are accelerated.
- *Experimenting* – Trying out new behaviors (approaches, ideas) to determine what is effective.
- *Performance Risk Taking* – Seeking new activities (tasks, assignments, roles) that provide opportunities to be challenged.
- *Interpersonal Risk Taking* – Discussing differences with others in ways that lead to learning and change.
- *Collaborating* – Finding ways to work with others that generate unique opportunities for learning.
- *Information Gathering* – Using various methods to remain current in one's area of expertise.
- *Feedback Seeking* – Asking others for feedback on one's ideas and overall performance.
- *Reflecting* – Slowing down to evaluate one's own performance to be more effective.

Dr. Warner Burke, the architect behind the Burke Learning Agility Self-Assessment, is quick to say his tool doesn't answer every question about learning agility. But it does give us something we've never had before: a clear definition of learning agility, nine measurable dimensions that capture how it shows up in action, and a practical way to identify both strengths and development areas.

This is powerful. For the first time, individuals can use concrete data to consciously leverage their learning agility—and pinpoint exactly where they need to grow. Before Burke's work, this kind of insight simply didn't exist. Other assessments have tried to capture learning agility, but under the scrutiny of industrial-organizational psychologists and HR professionals, they've come up short.

WHO CAN BENEFIT FROM A BETTER UNDERSTANDING OF LEARNING AGILITY?

At this point, you're probably wondering: **"How will a learning agility assessment actually help me?"** If you're an individual, the Burke Learning Agility Inventory can give you a clearer view of your strengths and areas for growth. Once you see where you stand—and if you agree the results feel accurate—the next step is to decide what you want to do with that insight. If you feel the effort required to change is greater than the payoff, you might decide to stay where you are. But it's also worth **Reflecting**: how could you better leverage your current strengths, and where could a little extra focus really move the needle?

If you lead a team or group, the Burke Learning Agility Inventory Self-Assessment becomes an even more powerful tool. It can help diagnose team dynamics—whether the group works together regularly or is coming together temporarily to solve a problem. When team members understand their own learning agility strengths and development needs, they're better positioned to contribute effectively and spot opportunities to grow. By looking at the team's collective learning agility profile, leaders can predict when the group will perform at its best and when it might hit roadblocks.

You can even use the information to structure the team more intentionally—for instance, assigning leadership roles based on individuals' unique learning agility strengths. At the same time, you can purposely assign employees to roles that challenge their weaker areas (like **Interpersonal Risk Taking** or **Collaborating**) with the understanding that their primary purpose is learning and growth. They'll still contribute, but they might listen more, ask more questions, and, yes, make some mistakes—which is all part of the learning process.

Learning agility also connects directly to how organizations tackle diversity. One dimension of learning agility is **Flexibility**—the ability to apply different frameworks or perspectives to a situation. Teams that are built with learning agility in mind can better harness the power of diversity, whether it's generational, cultural, gender-based, or otherwise. When team members can articulate their unique perspectives and stay open to others', the team's creativity, innovation, and performance are stronger. In some cases, a facilitator skilled in bringing out different voices can help teams get the most out of their diversity.

Monitoring how teams use both their learning agility strengths and their differences will ultimately determine their success.

For managers and supervisors, the benefits of the Burke Learning Agility Inventory extend even further. The results can inform critical conversations across learning and development, performance management, and succession planning. When used for development or performance reviews, it's about helping employees grow into more agile, adaptable learners. When used in succession planning, it's about identifying the people we want to bet on—the ones who can lead effectively no matter what the future holds. Because when it comes down to it, **more learning agile leaders are simply better equipped to succeed—whatever challenges come their way.**

HOW ORGANIZATIONS CAN BENEFIT FROM LEARNING AGILITY

When we talk about why learning agility matters, it's also worth asking: who stands to benefit the most from having a way to measure it? Startups, small businesses, and mid-size companies, in particular, can use learning agility assessments to better understand their high-potential talent and current leaders.

Speed and flexibility are natural strengths of smaller and growing companies. But like any strength, taken to an extreme, they can turn into weaknesses. Many fast-growing organizations move so quickly they skip the critical step of **Reflecting**—which means employees often repeat the same mistakes. In the rush to get things done, companies sometimes default to assigning tasks to the person who has "done it before," missing opportunities to stretch and develop other employees through **Performance Risk Taking** (with support and supervision).

If you're starting or scaling a business, it's the perfect time to bake learning agility into your culture—including your hiring process. For example, do you ask candidates to share a time they failed at work and what they learned from it? That's a real-world test of learning agility. If someone struggles to answer, it might signal they're not great at Reflecting—and may not have strong agile learning skills overall.

For new hires, understanding their learning agility profile can speed up onboarding. When employees quickly grasp how the organization works and how they learn best, they'll ramp up faster and perform better. They can even bring their results into conversations with their managers to shape assignments that foster growth.

Learning agility can also be woven into leadership training for new supervisors. Helping managers understand learning agility gives them a better framework for coaching and developing their teams. And for all employees, learning agility can become a valuable part of performance reviews and development planning.

Beyond individual development, organizations can also use the Burke Learning Agility Inventory Self-Assessment at a broader level. You might uncover learning agility strengths or gaps within certain departments, across teams, or between different business units. It can serve as a diagnostic tool to help integrate staff and line groups, bridge divides across business functions, or even understand differences between levels of leadership and geographic locations.

WHY LEARNING AGILITY WON'T ROCK THE BOAT

Rolling out learning agility assessments doesn't have to be disruptive. Adoption usually happens gradually, fueled by small experiments and early wins. That's an important reality to understand—and it's one of the key ways learning agility theory, especially the Burke Learning Agility Inventory, stands apart from other assessments.

Take Peter Senge's work in the late 20th century, for example. His influential book, *The Fifth Discipline* (published in 1990), made a strong case for building "learning organizations"—companies that systematically capture and share knowledge across the board. The idea was compelling, but it ran into a common organizational tension: autonomy versus conformity. Some companies fully embraced Senge's vision, investing heavily in centralized learning practices. Others tried, but ultimately pulled back, finding the financial and human costs too steep.

Knowledge management systems represent a more recent attempt to organize learning within organizations. While some companies have successfully built knowledge management into their DNA, the scale and investment needed are simply too big for most.

Here's the key difference between learning organizations, knowledge management, and learning agility: the first two are about **what** you know, while learning agility is about **how** you learn. Building a learning organization or rolling out a comprehensive knowledge management system demands full-scale, organization-wide commitment. Learning agility, on the other hand, is much more flexible. You can apply it at the individual, team, or full organizational level—whatever fits. That means you can run small pilots, experiment, and show real impact without needing to overhaul the whole company. It's easy to scale participation in learning agility assessments and tailor development to your organization's needs and size.

SO, WHERE DO WE GO FROM HERE?

In the next few chapters, Burke will break down the theory behind learning agility, walk you through the development of the Burke Learning Agility Inventory, share example results, and show you how to interpret them. Later, we'll dive into recognizing and building each learning agility dimension, and finally, we'll explore how to apply the Burke Learning Agility Inventory Self-Assessment across different areas of talent management.

CHAPTER 2

LEARNING AGILITY: A SUMMARY OF THEORY

"The ability to learn is a defining characteristic of being human; the ability to continue learning is an essential skill of leadership. When leaders lose that ability, they inevitably falter. When any of us lose that ability, we no longer grow."
(Bennis & Thomas, 2007, p. 1)

Attempting to learn about and measure learning agility is like using a yardstick when you are not sure that what you are measuring is a matter of inches and feet, linear, or even measurable at all. Yet it has been highly important for us to try. In this chapter, we will explore some of the research that has contributed to our current understanding of learning agility. We will also try to answer questions about how learning agility can improve the way we think about and measure effective leadership. Finally, we will discuss the impact of an organization's environment on learning agility.

LEARNING AGILITY AND LEADERSHIP: WHY DOES IT MATTER?

Chapter 1 discussed *Why Learning Agility and Why Now?* While we won't repeat that discussion, we will summarize a few key points here. For the past couple of decades, many researchers have noted that the ability to learn from experience is fundamental to leadership success. Some researchers have taken this idea further, suggesting that when selecting and developing leaders, we must consider not only their intelligence or technical competence, but also their ability to figure out what to do when they don't know what to do (Eichinger & Lombardo, 2004). Yet until recently, we did not have a reliable way to measure or test this idea, so it has gone largely unchecked in organizations today. We do not go so far as to declare learning agility as the answer to our leadership issues and failures, but we do think that with proper measurement and application, a contribution can be made to both theory and practice.

CURRENT STATE OF LEADERSHIP: WHAT GOT YOU HERE WILL NOT GET YOU THERE

Our primary interest in learning agility has been, and continues to be, within the context of leadership. The unfortunate reality is that nearly half of leaders fail, on average (Hogan, Hogan, & Kaiser, 2009). If we know this to be true, what is missing from our understanding of leadership? What are we doing wrong when it comes to selecting and developing leaders? We know that learning matters for effective leadership, yet many organizations overlook learning when selecting and growing their leaders. In fact, organizations typically select people for leadership who have strong technical skills and perhaps a good track record for performance, yet the relationship between technical ability and leadership success hovers around zero (Hogan, Curphy & Hogan, 1994). So perhaps we aren't looking at the right things, or at least *all* of the right things, when we choose leaders. Today's more advanced and complex leadership roles require new skills, abilities and perspectives, many of which must be learned as you go. This opens the door for learning agility to fill in at least some of the blanks in our understanding of leadership effectiveness.

Selection of leaders may not be the only area where we are not yet capturing the full picture of leadership success. When it comes to developing leaders, organizations still have a lot to learn as well. Researchers suggest that to the extent that leadership can be learned, it is learned through experience (McCall, 2010). Yet many organizations struggle to build effective learning opportunities, such as rotations and challenging assignments, into their employees' jobs. While executive decision makers may see the value in requiring new learning on the run, this type of development often takes a back seat to their preference for results and performance (McCall, 2010).

Many executives also subscribe to the belief that "the cream rises to the top" and that one's current expertise will somehow constitute future success. The reality, however, is that half of this "cream" lacks the proper consistency, let alone desirable taste, to succeed in today's ever-changing leadership roles. Why might these leaders be falling short? Individuals vary in their ability to learn from such experiences (Morrison & Brantner, 1992), making some leaders less able to apply learning to future challenges. It is clear that we need to find another lens through which we can select and develop leaders.

DEFINING AND MEASURING LEARNING AGILITY: WHAT'S BEEN DONE AND WHERE WE ARE NOW

In recent years, the concept of learning agility has become more popular among practitioners as a way to identify individual potential in organizational settings. An early definition of learning agility surfaced as "the willingness and ability to learn from experience, and subsequently apply that learning to perform successfully under new or first-time conditions" (Lombardo & Eichinger, 2000, p. 322). This concept captures an important aspect of what has been missing in the way we select and develop individuals in our organizations.

Several attempts have been made at developing a measure of learning agility or related concepts with varying degrees of scope and scientific or empirical rigor. Each of these has helped us better understand the concept of learning agility and how to measure it, but we believe a number of common limitations leave room for further development.

The most systematic of these measures, the Prospector® survey, was developed by Spreitzer, McCall and Mahoney (1997) to aid in the identification of international executive potential. While the Prospector survey is based on relevant literature, it does not explicitly measure the concept of learning agility. It does, however, capture potential through the measurement of an executive's ability to learn from experience. Researchers examined performance on "end-state," or "learning-oriented" competencies that they suggested are integral to executive performance: *Uses Feedback, Is Culturally Adventurous, Seeks Opportunities to Learn, Is Open to Criticism, Seeks Feedback,* and *Is Flexible.* In terms of results, only two of the six learning-oriented factors were shown to be significantly related to current performance evaluations, and learning-oriented factors were no more helpful in predicting performance than were end-state factors. The authors of the Prospector survey suggest this is because companies fail to take learning competencies into account when assessing performance (Spreitzer et al., 1997). This is likely true, but further evidence is needed to confirm the learning component of this measure. It is likely that the learning-oriented dimensions of the Prospector survey overlap significantly with learning agility; however, it cannot be assumed that the instrument adequately captures all aspects of learning agility.

Perhaps the first formal measure of learning agility was developed by Lombardo and Eichinger (2000) based on executive interviews and some early studies at the Center for Creative Leadership. The Choices Architect, as it was originally commercially branded, included four components, or factors, of learning agility termed mental agility, people agility, change agility and results agility. In contrast to the Prospector survey, the authors of the Choices Architect do claim to measure learning agility explicitly; but with 81 items comprising 27 dimensions, the instrument seems to measure more than just the construct in question. While the four factors possess intuitive appeal, their sheer scope suggests that a more focused measure may be needed.

Perhaps the most important contribution to the *Burke Learning Agility Self-Assessment*, in terms of providing a conceptual base for theory development and measurement, was the research of DeRue, Ashford and Myers in 2012. These authors reviewed the literature up to 2012 and defined learning agility primarily in terms of *Flexibility* and *Speed*. They also emphasized the importance of examining the relationship between learning agility and learning ability, while still distinguishing the two. For example, it may be that to be agile as a learner requires a basic amount of learning ability, but, after reaching a certain threshold of ability, there may be little relationship between ability and agility.

DeRue and his colleagues also provide a model for understanding important ingredients that affect learning agility. Their model includes antecedents, which is a word used to describe something that precedes something else. In this model, antecedents include individual differences such as *goal orientation, cognitive ability* and *openness to experience.* For example, according to this model, the extent to which a person is open to new experiences will be related to the person's level of learning agility. Contextual factors, which are often environmental in nature (such as organizational climate, culture and complexity in this model), are also thought to influence the relationship between one's learning agility and key outcomes. For example, the culture of the organization will greatly influence how, when and the extent to which learning agility is exhibited by employees. Finally, outcomes in this model include: (1) learning in and across situations, and (2) positive performance change over time. In other words, one's level of learning agility has an impact on how much one learns in a given situation and also how much one's performance changes over time.

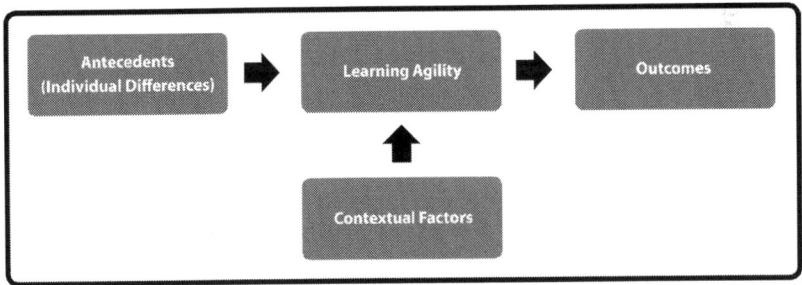

Figure 1: Abbreviated Version of the model by DeRue, Ashford and Myers (2012)

Development of the *Burke Learning Agility Inventory Self-Assessment* aligns closely with the work of DeRue and colleagues, particularly in the emphasis of **Flexibility** and **Speed**. However, our research departs in one key way. While DeRue's research states that learning agility can be understood in either of two processes—cognitive and behavioral—we have chosen to focus on behavioral approaches to measuring learning agility that are based solely on the premise that "if you can see it, you can measure it." By doing so, we believe that greater similarity in scores can be gained between multi-rater and self-assessments, and that raters may be better able to evaluate aspects of learning agility without needing an awareness of the construct.

In terms of where we landed, as presented in Chapter 1, the nine behaviorally based dimensions of learning agility assessed on the *Burke Learning Agility Inventory Self-Assessment* include:

- *Flexibility* – Being open to new ideas and proposing new solutions.
- *Speed* – Acting on ideas quickly so that those that aren't working are discarded and other possibilities are accelerated.
- *Experimenting* – Trying out new behaviors (approaches, ideas) to determine what is effective.
- *Performance Risk Taking* – Seeking new activities (tasks, assignments, roles) that provide opportunities to be challenged.
- *Interpersonal Risk Taking* – Discussing differences with others in ways that lead to learning and change.
- *Collaborating* – Finding ways to work with others that generate unique opportunities for learning.
- *Information Gathering* – Using various methods to remain current in one's area of expertise.
- *Feedback Seeking* – Asking others for feedback on one's ideas and overall performance.
- *Reflecting* – Slowing down to evaluate one's own performance to be more effective.

Chapter 3 will offer more detail in the research process/methodology that led to these nine dimensions.

A LITTLE BIT OF THEORY

At this point, you might be thinking, "Didn't we already cover the theory behind the *Burke Learning Agility Self-Assessment*?" You are correct in that we highlighted some key pieces of research that narrowed our approach for defining and measuring learning agility. But we need to take our discussion one step back to fully understand what learning agility is and where it fits into our understanding of human thought and behavior. For this, we need to examine learning agility theory in depth.

SOCIAL PSYCHOLOGY'S INFLUENCE ON LEARNING AGILITY: LEWIN'S FORMULATION

Considered by many to be "the father of social psychology," Lewin conceived of behavior as a function or interaction of the person with his or her environment. This is usually captured in the formula of $B = f(P, E)$ where B = behavior, P = person and E = environment. Lewin promoted this way of thinking as far back as the late 1930s and early '40s. Similarly, some social psychologists believe that behavior can *only* be explained interactively and not by either personality or environment alone. Likewise, in terms of cognition, this perspective believes that how someone thinks about a situation will determine how and whether that person will act. So according to Lewin, any action, whether observed behaviorally or merely a thought, is a perceptive interaction between the person and the situation. Thus, Lewin's formula integrates personality psychology and social psychology, which in turn establishes the theoretical basis for understanding learning agility: Agile learners have a deeper appreciation of the nature of social interaction and pay more attention to the consequences of their behavior, and at the same time, how they are affected by situations that they face. This awareness furnishes clues from which to learn.

LEARNING GOAL ORIENTATION'S INFLUENCE ON LEARNING AGILITY

Research suggests that individuals typically approach opportunities to achieve something as either a way to develop one's competence (a learning or mastery goal orientation) or to demonstrate one's competence (a performance goal orientation). Originating from work conducted by Carol Dweck (1986), these concepts have recently been applied to the workplace. Relevant to the concept of learning agility is the idea that goal orientations are associated with different personal beliefs about the relationship between effort and ability. Learning goal orientations are born from the belief that one's ability can be developed with effort and that this will lead to success. Conversely, performance goal orientations are born from the beliefs that one's ability is innate and difficult to develop. Therefore, effort is largely seen as unrelated to success.

Research has found that individuals can approach new and challenging experiences in different ways depending on their goal orientation. For example, individuals with a learning goal orientation display greater tolerance for ambiguity, thoughtfulness, open-mindedness (Kroll, 1988), show persistence in the face of difficulties (Dweck, 1986) and prefer challenging tasks (Ames & Archer, 1988). In contrast, performance goal orientations are negatively related to tolerance for ambiguity, thoughtfulness and complexity (Kroll, 1988), and have been shown to be related to a general avoidance of challenging tasks (Dweck, 1986).

What does all this mean for learning agility? Seeking out and being open to new and challenging experiences is important for any learning to be possible. So the specific behaviors that are related to learning goal orientation are likely to be integral to the concept of learning agility. Behaviors that demonstrate a tolerance for ambiguity, open-mindedness, persistence and a general preference for challenging tasks may increase the likelihood that individuals will find themselves in and persist with new experiences long enough for learning to occur. Further, individuals who continually seek new situations will have many experiences from which to extract understanding, meaning and insight. But, individuals who are unable to do this will likely avoid challenging situations, quit when difficulties arise, and perhaps continue to seek out familiar situations only. From this discussion, we conclude that a measure of learning agility should assess an individual tendency to behave in ways that align with a strong learning goal orientation.

ROLE OF ENVIRONMENT: JOB ADAPTABILITY'S
INFLUENCE ON LEARNING AGILITY

As discussed previously, the learning goal literature provides a rich source of behaviors that indicate an individual's ability to seek out and persist with new and challenging experiences. But, as Lewin's formula suggests, one must also consider the role of the environment when examining behaviors, including learning agility. That is, the extent to which the environment is conducive to learning, or is at least supportive of learning, will likely have an impact on how likely a person is to enact agile learning behaviors. For example, an environment that is conducive to learning and seeking out new experiences, and one which offers the ability to take in and manage information in an appropriate manner, will likely be sufficient for one to learn effectively. However, in many organizations the primary focus is on production rather than learning, which does not create optimal learning environments. In most work situations, immediate performance comes first while learning is of secondary concern, if a concern at all. For learning to occur during or after performance, an individual's ability to manage the immediate demands of the situation must be taken into consideration.

Job adaptability and performance literatures identify several behaviors that are relevant to job performance, including dealing with uncertain and unpredictable work situations and handling work stress. Pulakos, Arad, Donovan and Plamondon (2000) suggest that effective job performance requires an individual to be able to deal with uncertain and unpredictable work situations. They further note that individuals who do this well refuse to be paralyzed by uncertainty or ambiguity, don't need things to be black and white, and take effective action without having to know the total picture or have all the facts at hand. In order to learn from new experience, an individual will undoubtedly need to manage such uncertainty by displaying such behaviors.

Challenging situations, while rich opportunities for learning, can also evoke stress, especially in work situations where an individual is under pressure to deliver and be present in the moment. When not managed well, this pressure to deliver may impede an individual's ability to pay attention to cues, triggers or significant events that have the potential to provide valuable learning both during and after an experience. An individual's ability to handle such pressure is therefore an important aspect of the learning agility process. The work of Pulakos et al. (2000) again serves as a starting point for identifying behaviors that may demonstrate such ability. They suggest that effectively handling work stress involves remaining composed and cool when faced with difficult situations, managing frustration well by directing effort to constructive solutions rather than blaming others, and demonstrating resilience in stressful circumstances.

BUILDING ON THEORY: CONTRIBUTION OF BURKE LEARNING AGILITY INVENTORY SELF-ASSESSMENT REPORT RESEARCH

Agility, as extrapolated from DeRue et al. (2012), is defined to have two key components: *Flexibility* and *Speed*. The *Burke Learning Agility Self-Assessment* is built upon these two components defined as follows:

Flexibility. *Flexibility* is the process of abandoning behaviors that have worked in the past for new behaviors that meet the demands of the future. In this way, *Flexibility* involves unlearning as much as it does learning. Based on the needs of the current situation or environment and feedback from others, individuals change their course or approach to tasks.

Speed. *Speed* has to do with how quickly an individual can change course in behaviors, as well as how quickly an individual can read situational cues in order to form a plan of action. Colloquial phases such as "up to speed" and "quick study" exemplify the nature of this component of learning agility. Individuals who demonstrate behaviors related to *Speed* can change their position during a discussion in response to social cues, or immediately change behavior to adjust to the new knowledge.

With *Speed* and *Flexibility* as the backdrop, learning agility is defined as the engagement in learning behaviors to enhance the capacity to reconfigure activities quickly to meet the changing demands in the task environment.

In Chapter 3, we will explore the methodology by which our statistical analyses supported DeRue and colleagues' (2012) research demonstrating *Speed* and *Flexibility* as key dimensions of learning agility. We will also describe the process used to identify seven other dimensions of learning agility that, when practiced and incorporated into one's learning repertoire, support being flexible and quick.

Finally, as we will discuss in Chapter 3, learning agility is based on two major factors: skill and motivation. Skill concerns developing the 38 behaviors of the *Burke Learning Agility Inventory Self-Assessment*, while motivation is the willingness to take risks to move beyond one's comfort zone. The *Burke Learning Agility Inventory Self-Assessment* extends previous literature by taking both skill and motivation into account when developing and validating a practical, behavior-based measure of learning agility.

CHAPTER 3

HOW TO MEASURE LEARNING AGILITY: DEVELOPING THE BURKE LEARNING AGILITY ASSESSMENT

DEVELOPMENT OF THE BURKE LEARNING AGILITY INVENTORY™

Based on a review of research included in Chapter 2 and preliminary testing, a 38-item learning agility inventory was created for further investigation. It included a seven-point rating scale, ranging from 1 for "Not at All" to 7 for "Very Frequently." The assessment was given the name *Burke Learning Agility Inventory*. Initial research suggested that learning agility consists of nine relatively independent dimensions. We've mentioned them earlier, but they bear repeating:

- *Flexibility* – Being open to new ideas and proposing new solutions.
- *Speed* – Acting on ideas quickly so that those not working are discarded and other possibilities are accelerated.
- *Experimenting* – Trying out new behaviors (approaches, ideas) to determine what is effective.
- *Performance Risk Taking* – Seeking new activities (tasks, assignments, roles) that provide opportunities to be challenged.
- *Interpersonal Risk Taking* – Discussing differences with others in ways that lead to learning and change.

- *Collaborating* – Finding ways to work with others that generate unique opportunities for learning.
- *Information Gathering* – Using various methods to remain current in one's area of expertise.
- *Feedback Seeking* – Asking others for feedback on one's ideas and overall performance.
- *Reflecting* – Slowing down to evaluate one's own performance to be more effective.

RESEARCH SAMPLES: TESTING THE BURKE LEARNING AGILITY SELF-ASSESSMENT REPORT IN DIFFERENT POPULATIONS

Within a four-year period, the 38-item *Burke Learning Agility Self-Assessment* was administered to three sample groups. A summary of the sample groups is provided here.

MID-LEVEL MANAGERS

Participants for this study received an email through a list server that included alumni of executive education programs at a large, Mid-Atlantic organization that specializes in leadership development. In total, 393 participants completed the study materials; 57% of the participants were male, with the largest proportion, 27%, being between the ages of 35 to 44. The age breakdown for the remainder of this group was 45 to 49 years old (19%), 50 to 54 years old (18%), and 55 to 64 years old (18%). The majority of participants, 57%, held jobs in the corporate sector and came from various roles in the organization. These included manager (24%), director (19%), professional staff (13%) and executive level (11%).

ONLINE CONVENIENCE SAMPLE

A convenience sample of 207 individuals was recruited using Amazon's Mechanical Turk survey service. Participation was limited to U.S. adults over the age of 18. Slightly more than half of participants, or 51.2%, were male. The majority of the sample was white/Caucasian at 71.5%. The racial breakdown for the rest of the sample was as follows: 7.7% Asian/Asian-American, 6.8% Hispanic/Latino(a), 5.3% black/African-American, and 1.9% biracial; 6.8% of the people surveyed did not respond to the question. The average age of participants was 34 (SD=10.25), and as a group they had an average of 13.86 years of work experience (SD=9.63). More than one-third of participants, 34.3%, had completed a degree at a four-year college. Almost one quarter of participants, 24.2%, reported completing some college, while 13% had completed a high school diploma or GED degree, 12.6% had completed a two-year college degree, 7.7% had completed a master's degree, and 1.4% had completed a professional degree such as a medical degree (MD) or juris doctor (JD).

HEALTH CARE ORGANIZATION SAMPLE

A sample of 471 employees at a health care organization was surveyed using an online survey platform. Slightly more than half of participants were female (56.1%), 14.4% were male, and 29.5% did not respond to the question. The majority of the sample, 60%, were white/Caucasian. The remainder of the survey respondents identified themselves as follows: 6% Hispanic/Latino(a), 1.7% Asian/Asian-American, 1.5% black/African-American, 9% biracial or multiracial, 0.6% Native Hawaiian/Pacific Islander, and 29.5% did not respond to the question. The average age of participants was 41.11 years (SD=14.10), with an average of 20.29 years of formal work experience (SD=13.38). Roughly one-quarter (26%) of participants had earned a four-year college degree; another 19.1% had earned a two-year college degree, 14.2% had completed some college, 5.4% had earned a high school diploma or GED, 2.2% had earned a master's degree, 3.4% had earned a professional degree such as a medical degree (MD) or juris doctor (JD), and 0.2% completed a doctorate program. The question about education was not answered by 29.5% of participants.

RESEARCH RESULTS

When developing any assessment, researchers must gather data to confirm that the assessment is reliable, meaning that it provides consistent results under consistent conditions, and valid, meaning that it measures what it intends to measure.

Results from all three studies demonstrate that the *Burke Learning Agility Inventory Self-Assessment* is indeed reliable. Since there are I-O psychologists and researchers among us, I'll refer to Cronbach's alpha, a correlational statistic that demonstrates the extent to which each item of a scale clusters together; the higher the alpha the stronger the scale regarding clustering. For the *Burke Learning Agility Inventory Self-Assessment*, the Cronbach's alphas are greater than 0.7, as shown in Table 1. The table shows excellent scale reliability, or internal consistency, for each of the *Burke Learning Agility Self-Assessment* subscales in all three samples. With this information, we conclude that the *Burke Learning Agility Self-Assessment* is a reliable measure for use across multiple types of samples.

TABLE 1. RELIABILITY RESULTS: INTERNAL CONSISTENCY

Scale	Item Count	Cronbach's Alpha by Sample		
		Sample 1	Sample 2	Sample 3
Flexibility	5	.81	.80	.79
Speed	5	.85	.89	.90
Experimenting	4	.85	.85	.85
Performance Risk Taking	4	.88	.90	.86
Interpersonal Risk Taking	4	.78	.79	.76
Collaborating	4	.88	.82	.80
Information Gathering	4	.81	.87	.86
Feedback Seeking	4	.87	.88	.86
Reflecting	4	.83	.87	.88

Sample 1: N=393; Sample 2: N = 193-195*; Sample 3: N = 279-280* (*some missing data)

Of course, establishing that a test is valid is just as important as determining its reliability, as validity shows that we are measuring what we say we are measuring. To establish evidence of validity, researchers examine intercorrelations, which show the relationships between the dimensions, ranging from 0 for no relationship to 1 for 100% related. The intercorrelations of the *Burke Learning Agility Self-Assessment* scales for the mid-level

TABLE 2. BURKE LEARNING AGILITY SELF-ASSESSMENT REPORT DIMENSION INTERCORRELATIONS (ACROSS SAMPLES)

	Collaborating	Experimenting	Feedback Seeking	Interpersonal Risk Taking	Information Gathering	Performance Risk Taking	Reflecting	Speed	Flexibility
Collaborating									
Experimenting	.69** .58** .47**								
Feedback Seeking	.59** .56** .48**	.55** .51** .45**							
Interpersonal Risk Taking	.72** .51** .39**	.68** .62** .43**	.67** .54** .41*						
Information Gathering	.72** .59** .39**	.73** .59** .37**	.58** .57** .34**	.71** .50** .24**					
Performance Risk Taking	.67** .62** .52**	.63** .65** .60**	.56** .55** .58**	.67** .59** .41**	.66** .61** .41**				
Reflecting	.75** .55** .46**	.70** .66** .53**	.62** .55** .39**	.72** .54** .45**	.64** .63** .42**	.65** .52** .48**			
Speed	.52** .48** .50**	.60** .57** .53**	.34** .40** .29**	.51** .50** .29**	.57** .51** .33**	.47** .47** .45**	.53** .50** .43**		
Flexibility	.72** .68** .56**	.71** .74** .61**	.46** .52** .52*	.63** .60** .41*	.66** .66** .40**	.60** .68** .62**	.69** .64** .57**	.74** .59** .52**	

Sample 1: N=393; Sample 2: N = 193-195*; Sample 3: N = 279-280* (*some missing data)

manager sample, the online convenience sample, and the health care organization sample appear in the table that follows. Intercorrelations between dimensions are moderate and positively correlated, which is consistent with what we know about learning agility based on the theory presented in Chapter 2. It is also important to note that the moderate intercorrelations found—those that are less than 0.8—indicate that while scales are related, they are also measuring unique dimensions. This provides further support for the nine unique dimensions of learning agility tested.

WHAT THESE NUMBERS TELL US ABOUT LEARNING AGILITY

From the reliability and validity data presented here, we know that we are measuring the right things and measuring them consistently. This is an important first step in establishing the usefulness of a tool like the *Burke Learning Agility Inventory Self-Assessment*. Additional statistical analyses performed are detailed in the *Burke Learning Agility Inventory Technical Report* (2016). The Tech Report was updated/amended in 2018 and 2024. For example, a confirmatory factor analysis was conducted. As expected, results of this analysis demonstrated that all of the dimensions related to one another in people's minds as they answered each of the questions. That is, they "hung together" from a statistical perspective, which provided further evidence that the *Burke Learning Agility Self-Assessment* is in fact measuring one construct, which we call learning agility.

Another way to demonstrate effectiveness of a measure, as detailed in the technical report, is to gather evidence of convergent and discriminant validity. In this way, results of statistical analysis showed that learning agility as measured on the *Burke Learning Agility Inventory Self-Assessment* correlated with concepts that we expected it should (for example, resistance to change and learning goal orientation) but were uncorrelated with concepts that were not expected to be related (for example, risk aversion and reactance). This is one more way to demonstrate that the *Burke Learning Agility Inventory Self-Assessment* is really measuring learning agility, as defined by the nine dimensions it includes.

Chapter 4 will include a sample *Burke Learning Agility Self-Assessment* report, and will show how results and recommendations for becoming more learning agile are presented.

CHAPTER 4

INTERPRETING THE *BURKE LEARNING AGILITY SELF-ASSESSMENT REPORT*

This chapter contains an actual sample report that is produced when an individual completes the *Burke Learning Agility Inventory Self-Report*. Page 36 is the title page of the report. Page 37 shows the report's Table of Contents. Page 38 shows a couple of introductory paragraphs on the assessment report. Page 40 lists each of the nine dimensions with their definitions. Page 41 shows a person's Overall and Dimension Scores expressed as percentiles. The next 27 pages, 42–68, show each of the nine dimensions expressed as percentiles. Each dimension lists each of the corresponding behaviors expressed as below average, average, or above average followed by a description of how a person can improve. The next four pages, 69–72 provide a person's highest and lowest item scores and pages to create a development plan. This is the final chapter in Section 1 of the book. In Section 2 we will look at each of the dimensions in more depth. There is a separate chapter for each dimension.

The Learning Agility Inventory

Introduction	3
How to Interpret Your Results	4
Defining Burke's Dimensions	5
Overall Results	6
Flexibility	7
Speed	10
Experimenting	13
Performance Risk Taking	16
Interpersonal Risk Taking	19
Collaborating	22
Information Gathering	25
Feedback Seeking	28
Reflecting	31
Summary of Scores	34
Action Plan	36

ƎB

Introduction

In today's fast-paced world of constant change and disruption, Learning Agility has emerged as a crucial superpower for both individuals and organizations. While knowledge is more accessible than ever, skills that were once vital can quickly become outdated, replaced by the evolving demands of a rapidly changing landscape.

Emeritus Columbia University Professor Warner Burke's groundbreaking research identified 9 dimensions and 38 behaviors essential for enhancing **Learning Agility**—the ability to adapt, learn, and apply new skills and knowledge with speed and effectiveness. Building on this research, Burke and his team at Columbia University developed the Burke Learning Agility Inventory™. This powerful methodology provides a clear framework to measure and cultivate Learning Agility, enabling individuals to thrive in dynamic environments.

The assessment is your starting point on the journey to staying ahead in a world where the ability to learn faster and more effectively is your greatest competitive advantage. It examines your Learning Agility across nine dimensions, comparing your results to the norms established by Burke's research.

No matter where you stand today, there's always room for growth. The key lies in understanding which specific skills and behaviors to prioritize for development. This report provides valuable insights into your current strengths and offers targeted recommendations to help you expand your Learning Agility and unlock your full potential.

This report is brought to you by Burke Assessments, LLC.

How to Interpret Your Results

To help you understand your feedback, your scores have been compared to a large normative database of individuals who have completed the Burke Learning Assessment Inventory™.

You will receive scores expressed in terms of percentiles. For example, if you have a score at 80th, 20% of the people scored higher than you. In this report, you will find the following percentile scores ranked against the norm group:

In this report, you will find the following percentile scores ranked against the norm group:

- Your overall Learning Agility result
- Your results by Dimension
- Your results by Behavior

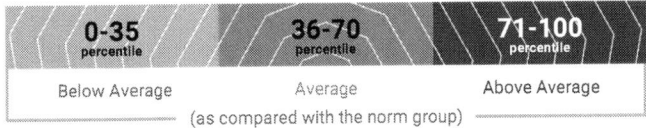

0-35 percentile	36-70 percentile	71-100 percentile
Below Average	Average	Above Average

(as compared with the norm group)

Defining Burke's Dimensions

1.

Flexibility

Being open to new ideas and proposing new solutions.

2.

Speed

Acting on ideas quickly so that those not working are discarded and other possibilities are accelerated.

3.

Experimenting

Trying out new behaviors (i.e., approaches, ideas) to determine what is effective.

4.

Performance Risk Taking

Seeking new activities (i.e., tasks, assignments, roles) that provide opportunities to be challenged.

5.

Interpersonal Risk Taking

Confronting differences with others in ways that lead to learning and change.

6.

Collaborating

Finding ways to work with others that generate unique opportunities for learning.

7.

Information Gathering

Using various methods to remain current in one's area of expertise.

8.

Feedback Seeking

Asking others for feedback on one's ideas and overall performance.

9.

Reflecting

Slowing down to evaluate one's own performance in order to be more effective.

ƐB

Overall Results

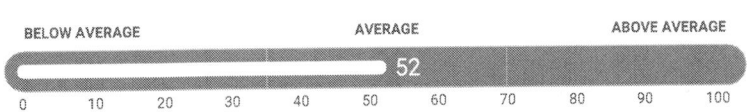

BELOW AVERAGE	AVERAGE	ABOVE AVERAGE

52

0   10   20   30   40   50   60   70   80   90   100

Overall Score Interpretation

Your score, at the 52nd percentile, reflects a solid average score as compared to the norm (comparison) group indicated above. Compared with peers from this group, you display a good level of flexibility, skills, and motivation. Your capacity to apply agile behavior in learning situations is consistent, and with just a bit more focus, you can further enhance your agility and adaptability.

Subscale Scores

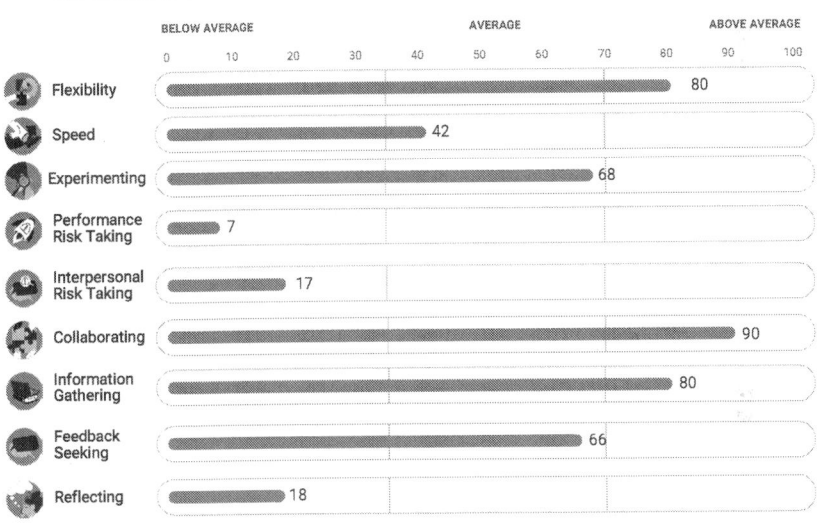

	BELOW AVERAGE	AVERAGE	ABOVE AVERAGE
Flexibility			80
Speed	42		
Experimenting		68	
Performance Risk Taking	7		
Interpersonal Risk Taking	17		
Collaborating			90
Information Gathering		80	
Feedback Seeking	66		
Reflecting	18		

BD

FLEXIBILITY

Being open to new ideas and proposing new solutions.

Your Overall Score: 80

BELOW AVERAGE	AVERAGE	ABOVE AVERAGE

80

0   10   20   30   40   50   60   70   80   90   100

Flexibility involves regularly bringing fresh ideas to the conversation and proposing creative solutions. Your above-average score in this area suggests you often contribute ideas that add significant value to your team and environment. Colleagues likely see you as someone who frequently sparks innovation and drives positive change.

You often explore a wide range of options before making decisions. By consistently presenting multiple solutions, you stimulate others to think beyond conventional approaches and tackle challenges with greater creativity and openness.

In today's fast-paced and ever-evolving world, your ability to frequently adapt and refocus quickly is a highly valuable strength.

You regularly find common ground amidst differing perspectives, which is a key strength in leadership. Your openness to diverse viewpoints, even those that differ from your original stance, is a recurring demonstration of your ability to understand, express, and champion new ideas.

You consistently examine and identify differences among points of view, rather than focusing on similarities you're already familiar with. Differences provide valuable insights for a deeper understanding of complex issues, effectiveness, and for innovation.

By intentionally practicing the five behaviors of flexibility, you'll strengthen your position as an influential leader who can navigate challenges while creating meaningful value.

FLEXIBILITY

		Norm Group
Behavior 1	Propose innovative solutions	ABOVE AVERAGE
Behavior 2	Consider options before acting	BELOW AVERAGE
Behavior 3	Switch between different jobs/tasks	AVERAGE
Behavior 4	Find common themes among opposing points of view	ABOVE AVERAGE
Behavior 5	Articulate different ideas/perspectives	ABOVE AVERAGE

80

Additional Development Recommendations

- Embrace and promote technological innovation in your work, such as AI – not only as a critical step to staying ahead, but also as a powerful exercise in mastering flexibility.

- Develop ambidexterity—the balance between long-term strategic vision and short-term execution—can help you lead even more effectively and navigate complex priorities with confidence.

- Engage in complex scenario planning exercises. Consider worst-case scenarios or highly unlikely events and develop detailed response plans. This will challenge your adaptability and strategic thinking.

- If possible, seek opportunities to work on international cross functional projects or with global teams. Adapting to different cultures, time zones, and working styles will further enhance your flexibility.

8B

SPEED

Acting on ideas quickly so that those not working
are discarded and other possibilities are accelerated.

Your Overall Score: 42

BELOW AVERAGE	AVERAGE	ABOVE AVERAGE

42

0   10   20   30   40   50   60   70   80   90   100

Speed involves trying new behaviors quickly and learning from mistakes without dwelling on failure, moving swiftly to the next attempt . While you occasionally demonstrate a good balance between speed and thoroughness to maximize impact, there is room for growth in this area.

Sometimes it may take you longer to become effective in new initiatives, although you typically manage to get up to speed within a reasonable timeframe. Enhancing your ability to learn and integrate experiences more rapidly and accurately will strengthen your capacity to contribute to projects with greater impact.

At times, you quickly and efficiently grasp new ideas and concepts. However, you may occasionally get caught up in details or follow tangents, which can slow progress.

While you sometimes acquire new skills at a reasonable pace, it seems that your speed not be as fast as expected. By continuing to build on this strength, you can further enhance your overall contribution across diverse situations.

Handling unexpected challenges with composure and effectiveness is something you occasionally do, but it's possible that these situations often become emotionally taxing for you. To mitigate this, focus on cultivating a proactive mindset by these strategies will help you remain focused and maintain efficiency, even under pressure.

SPEED

		Norm Group
Behavior 6	Quickly develop solutions	AVERAGE
Behavior 7	Get up to speed in new projects/tasks	BELOW AVERAGE
Behavior 8	Readily grasp new ideas/concepts	AVERAGE
Behavior 9	Acquire new skills and knowledge rapidly	AVERAGE
Behavior 10	React well to unexpected problems	BELOW AVERAGE

42

Additional Development Recommendations

- Network with peers both inside and outside your organization to swiftly identify techniques and approaches that can speed up your efforts.

- Jump into new initiatives where quick learning and rapid adaptation are crucial. Look for fast-paced environments that push you to quickly develop and apply your skills.

- Develop strategies to stay focused and avoid getting bogged down by less important details, ensuring swift and efficient progress.

- Create a feedback mechanism that quickly reviews actions and results, allowing for immediate improvements and adjustments.

- Read "Thinking, Fast and Slow" by Daniel Kahneman and absorb insights from this book to enhance your quick decision-making and agile thinking.

ℬB

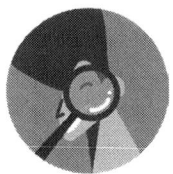

EXPERIMENTING

Trying out new behaviors (i.e., approaches, ideas) to determine what is effective.

Your Overall Score: 68

BELOW AVERAGE	AVERAGE	ABOVE AVERAGE

68

0   10   20   30   40   50   60   70   80   90   100

Scoring average on Experimenting suggests you occasionally show a willingness to explore a wide range of new strategies to address situations in addition to drawing on your past experiences. This is a valuable balance that fosters innovation. Expanding this approach further could greatly enhance your professional growth and impact.

Testing ideas, whether they are obvious or a bit of a stretch, is an important aspect of learning agility. Scoring average on this dimension suggests that increasing the pace of experimenting with new ideas could enhance your learning agility. Additionally, sharing unconventional ideas with others can stimulate further thinking and lead to valuable new insights. Embracing a culture of experimentation and open-mindedness will drive continuous learning and improvement.

You occasionally experiment with different approaches to solve problems, and that suggests others on your team or in projects recognize and appreciate this quality. Playing this role consistently will position you as a valuable contributor to innovation and progress. People often admire your willingness to test and refine ideas, as it encourages improvement and inspires others to think creatively.

At times, you use a trial-and-error approach in your work. This contribution may inspire others who are less willing to make mistakes. Eliminating options through trial and error, may at times seem tedious and time consuming but necessary to gaining support for new ideas. By using this methodical approach, you can help accelerate innovation in your environment.

EXPERIMENTING

		Norm Group
Behavior 11	Evaluate new ways of solving problems	ABOVE AVERAGE
Behavior 12	Experiment with unproven ideas	BELOW AVERAGE
Behavior 13	Try different approaches	AVERAGE
Behavior 14	Learn by trial and error	AVERAGE

68

Additional Development Recommendations

- Read "Mindset: The New Psychology of Success" by Carol Dweck to gain insights on how to develop a growth mindset from this renowned book by the American psychologist.

- Embrace a Growth Mindset by cultivating an attitude that values learning from mistakes and views failure as a steppingstone to success. This mindset will encourage you to try new things without fear of failure.

- Identify a Mentor, within or outside your organization who engages in similar experimental activities to discuss successes and challenges.

- Review a project you led where the results could have been better. Analyze which experimental techniques were effective and why. Consider additional techniques that could have been used and how. Apply these learnings to future projects.

BB

Performance Risk Taking

PERFORMANCE RISK TAKING

Seeking new activities (i.e., tasks, assignments, roles)
that provide opportunities to be challenged.

Your Overall Score: 7

BELOW AVERAGE	AVERAGE	ABOVE AVERAGE

```
          7
0    10    20    30    40    50    60    70    80    90    100
```

Taking performance risks means stepping out of your comfort zone and taking calculated actions to facilitate learning and growth. Scoring low in this area suggests that you rarely seek opportunities that challenge you beyond your current comfort zone. Developing this capability could significantly enhance your confidence and ability to take on and excel in new challenges.

You may not often demonstrate the ability to navigate complex situations that lack clear direction. While this is an important skill, taking more calculated risks with challenging or ambiguous assignments could help you build greater learning agility and make a stronger impact in your role. To reduce uncertainty and improve decision-making, focus on gathering and analyzing critical information from diverse sources that clarify the approach and increase your confidence.

Taking on challenging or risky assignments may be something you seldom do, limiting your opportunity to develop your ability to assess, mitigate, and manage potential risks effectively. Starting with smaller, manageable risks can help build your confidence and gradually prepare for more complex challenges over time.

Scoring low in this dimension suggests you rarely volunteer for assignments with a potential risk of failure. Embrace the learning opportunity by giving yourself permission to take risks and potentially fail on a task. However, it is essential to reflect on and describe what you have learned from the experience and identify what you will do differently next time. Look for opportunities to try again, either within the current project or in a new context, as soon as possible. This approach fosters continuous growth and improvement.

PERFORMANCE RISK TAKING

Norm Group

7	Behavior 15	Take on challenging roles	BELOW AVERAGE
	Behavior 16	Engage in ambiguous tasks	BELOW AVERAGE
	Behavior 17	Embrace work that is risky	BELOW AVERAGE
	Behavior 18	Volunteer for projects that involve the possibility of failure	BELOW AVERAGE

Additional Development Recommendations

- Surround yourself with supportive colleagues and mentors who can provide guidance and encouragement as you start taking risks.

- Begin by taking risks in low-stakes situations where the consequences are minimal. This will help you build confidence without feeling overwhelmed.

- Acknowledge and celebrate even the smallest successes in your risk-taking efforts. Positive reinforcement can boost your confidence and encourage you to take greater risks.

- Try to be part of projects, which may hold the possibility of failure. Discuss the project's potential risks with your supervisor or a knowledgeable colleague. Both of you should independently assess the risks, share your perspectives, listen to their feedback, and collaborate on strategies to minimize them.

Interpersonal Risk Taking

INTERPERSONAL RISK TAKING

Confronting differences with others in ways that lead to learning and change.

Your Overall Score: 17

BELOW AVERAGE	AVERAGE	ABOVE AVERAGE

17

0   10   20   30   40   50   60   70   80   90   100

Interpersonal risk-taking is about addressing differences with others in ways that promote growth and positive change.

Your low score on this dimension indicates that raising difficult or uncomfortable issues with others may be challenging for you. This skill is valuable in interactions with both individuals and groups. By describing an issue or problem neutrally and explaining its impact on performance, you can help facilitate improvement.

When it comes to seeking help, you seem to find it difficult to ask for support. Many people feel unsure if their request for help will be well received or see asking for help as a sign of weakness. The response you get from others by being vulnerable will surprise you and give you confidence to make this request in the future.

Discussing your mistakes openly may also be an area for growth. Mistakes are a natural part of the learning process, and without making them when trying new behaviors, you might not be taking enough risks. Clearly articulating what you learned and what you will do differently next time can ensure growth from these experiences.

Interpersonal risk-taking also involves expressing opinions that differ from the group. Stepping out of your comfort zone and being vulnerable are key aspects of this and your score indicates this is might be difficult for you. Supporting your position with facts or other information can encourage the group to reconsider its stance.

INTERPERSONAL RISK TAKING

Norm Group

17

Behavior 19	Bring up tough issues with others	BELOW AVERAGE
Behavior 20	Ask others for help	BELOW AVERAGE
Behavior 21	Discuss mistakes with others	AVERAGE
Behavior 22	Challenge other's ideas that are shared by many	BELOW AVERAGE

Additional Development Recommendations

- Surround yourself with supportive colleagues and mentors who encourage you to take interpersonal risks and provide guidance when needed. This can help build foundational skills and promote growth.

- Begin by initiating low-stakes conversations with colleagues to build confidence. Gradually work your way up to more challenging interactions. Over time, this will enhance your ability to take interpersonal risks more comfortably.

- After taking an interpersonal risk, reflect on the positive outcomes and what you learned from the experience. This can boost your confidence and motivate you to take greater risks in the future.

- Start with small, supportive interactions to address the fear of rejection. Over time, this will enhance the ability to take interpersonal risks more comfortably.

⅋B

COLLABORATING

Your Overall Score: 90

BELOW AVERAGE				AVERAGE				ABOVE AVERAGE	

90

0	10	20	30	40	50	60	70	80	90	100

Collaborating in learning agility means finding ways to work with others and/or generating unique opportunities for learning. Scoring high in this area demonstrates that you consistently leverage the expertise of others to create meaningful learning opportunities. You frequently seek input, share knowledge, and engage with others to drive innovation and achieve shared goals. Your ability to collaborate effectively positions you as a valuable contributor to team success and organizational growth.

You actively and consistently collaborate with colleagues from diverse backgrounds, seeking out those who think differently and bring unique perspectives. You understand the value of engaging with individuals across various roles, departments, and cultural backgrounds. Your commitment to practicing active listening and curiosity helps foster richer discussions, build mutual respect, and generate innovative solutions.

By encouraging diverse viewpoints, you enhance team dynamics and overall effectiveness.Working across teams and departments regularly demonstrates your ability to build strong relationships beyond your immediate sphere. Your collaborative approach enables you to uncover new opportunities for growth and make meaningful contributions to organizational goals. Whether participating in cross-functional projects or leading collaborative efforts, you embrace opportunities to expand your network and create value across different areas of the organization.

Proactively seeking input, feedback, and viewpoints from stakeholders with a vested interest in issues, you recognize the critical role of diverse perspectives in achieving better outcomes. By asking thoughtful questions and inviting constructive dialogue, you create an environment where differing opinions are not only welcomed but celebrated. This consistent behavior strengthens your confidence, enhances decision-making, and inspires others to adopt a more collaborative mindset.

COLLABORATING

Norm Group

Behavior 23	Leverage skills, knowledge, and talent of others	ABOVE AVERAGE
Behavior 24	Work with colleagues from different backgrounds	ABOVE AVERAGE
Behavior 25	Collaborate with other parts of the organization	ABOVE AVERAGE
Behavior 26	Ask stakeholders for their point of view	ABOVE AVERAGE

90

Additional Development Recommendations

- Enhance Your Cultural Intelligence: Take a course in cultural intelligence to strengthen your ability to lead and collaborate with people from diverse backgrounds, enriching both your personal and professional growth.

- Seek Cross-Functional Opportunities: Look for projects or initiatives that involve multiple areas of the organization, helping you broaden your perspective and foster collaboration across teams.

- Actively participate in knowledge-sharing activities outside your area of expertise, such as team meetings, brainstorming sessions, or collaborative workshops, to learn from others and contribute new ideas.

- Expand Your Professional Network: Consider joining a local or national professional organization in your field to connect with a diverse range of individuals, building a broader and more supportive network.

ꓯB

INFORMATION GATHERING

Your Overall Score: 80

BELOW AVERAGE			AVERAGE			ABOVE AVERAGE	

80

0   10   20   30   40   50   60   70   80   90   100

Information gathering in learning agility is all about staying ahead of trends and developments in your area of expertise. In today's fast-changing world, your ability to consistently stay informed demonstrates a high level of dedication and effort.

Scoring above average in this area highlights your proactive approach to staying current on industry trends, research, and new insights. You regularly seek out the latest developments and integrate this knowledge into your work, ensuring you remain a valuable and forward-thinking contributor in your field. This not only enhances your performance but also inspires those around you to stay informed and continually improve.

Whether through reading, exploring diverse mediums, or pursuing ongoing learning opportunities, you consistently gather valuable information to fuel your growth. You have a natural ability to identify the most relevant and impactful data, which allows you to guide your decisions and next steps with clarity and confidence. This skill helps you navigate complex challenges and seize opportunities that others might overlook.

Attending formal training or education seems important to you and you seem to use these opportunities as a way to improve your skills. The payoff will be in how you implement what you learn in your role at work. Try to identify a learning partner who can help you monitor your success in applying what you have learned.

INFORMATION GATHERING

		Norm Group
Behavior 27	Seek new information on topics related to your own field	ABOVE AVERAGE
Behavior 28	Update knowledge through training and education	ABOVE AVERAGE
Behavior 29	Read books, journals, blogs, articles, etc. to stay informed	AVERAGE
Behavior 30	Collect data to increase knowledge and inform next steps	ABOVE AVERAGE

80

Additional Development Recommendations

- Start learning how to use AI tools to collect, store, and analyze data. This will streamline your research and enhance your ability to make data-driven decisions.

- Broaden the range of sources you use to gather information. Explore new journals, podcasts, webinars, and online courses to ensure a diverse and comprehensive understanding of your field.

- Participate in conferences and seminars relevant to your industry. These events provide opportunities to learn about the latest trends, network with experts, and gain new insights that can enhance your knowledge base.

- Set up a platform within your organization, such as a newsletter or internal blog, where you can share the latest research, trends, and insights with your colleagues. This fosters a culture of continuous learning and keeps everyone informed.

ƎB

FEEDBACK SEEKING

Your Overall Score: 66

BELOW AVERAGE   AVERAGE   ABOVE AVERAGE

66

0   10   20   30   40   50   60   70   80   90   100

Asking for feedback is a powerful driver of professional growth, offering insights into your performance and helping you identify opportunities to refine your skills. Scoring average in this area suggests that you sometimes seek feedback, which might limit your ability to fully capitalize on the benefits it provides for personal and professional development.

You at times seek guidance or constructive input from peers, leaders, or senior professionals. While you occasionally request feedback when prompted or in specific situations. Developing a more consistent approach could help you stay better aligned with expectations and demonstrate a stronger commitment to personal improvement.

Conversations with your leader or mentors about career growth and development opportunities happens from time to time,, which could result in missed opportunities to gain clarity on your goals, or the steps needed to achieve them.

You once in a while seek the opinions of colleagues, which may limit your opportunities to uncover areas for improvement. Making feedback a more regular part of your routine can help you build trust, enhance your decision-making, and foster continuous learning.

FEEDBACK SEEKING

Norm Group

Behavior 31	Ask peers for feedback on performance	ABOVE AVERAGE
Behavior 32	Seek feedback from manager	AVERAGE
Behavior 33	Discuss potential advancement with manager	AVERAGE
Behavior 34	Ask others how to improve performance	AVERAGE

66

Additional Development Recommendations

- Set up regular one-on-one meetings with your manager or mentor to discuss your performance and seek constructive feedback. This helps you stay aligned with expectations and identify areas for improvement.

- Engage in peer review sessions where you and your colleagues can provide feedback to each other. This encourages a culture of openness and helps you gain insights from different perspectives.

- When seeking feedback, ask specific questions about your performance (what and how). This can help you get targeted feedback that is more actionable and relevant.

- Take time to reflect on the feedback you receive and consider how you can apply it to your work. Implementing changes based on feedback shows your commitment to continuous improvement.

- Discuss future career opportunities with your supervisor and the steps needed to be prepared. If necessary take the initiative to start this conversation.

ƆB

Reflecting

REFLECTING

Your Overall Score: 18

BELOW AVERAGE	AVERAGE	ABOVE AVERAGE

18

0   10   20   30   40   50   60   70   80   90   100

Reflection in learning agility means taking a moment to evaluate your performance, strategies, and decisions to grow and become more effective. Scoring low in this area suggests that you rarely use this practice. Developing a habit of reflection can greatly enhance your ability to turn experiences into actionable insights for personal and professional growth.

You may often skip analyzing the causes or potential outcomes of decisions, making it harder to anticipate challenges or identify ways to improve. Pausing before or after key decisions to uncover valuable insights can help guide future actions. Building this habit gradually, such as reflecting on one decision or project per week, can significantly enhance your ability to navigate complex situations.

It seems you seldom engage in collaborative reflection with others, leading to missed opportunities for gaining deeper insights from shared experiences. Actively seeking input from others or inviting discussions after completing projects or initiatives can offer a better understanding of different perspectives and foster shared learning.

Reviewing and evaluating completed tasks or initiatives is infrequently part of your approach, which might hinder your ability to recognize successes or identify areas for improvement. By making a conscious effort to review your work more systematically, even starting with smaller tasks, you can gradually build this habit. Over time, this practice will help you refine your methods, improve outcomes, and position yourself for greater success in a dynamic professional environment.

REFLECTING

		Norm Group
Behavior 35	Reflect on work processes and projects	BELOW AVERAGE
Behavior 36	Reflect on how to be more effective	BELOW AVERAGE
Behavior 37	Consider reasons for and consequences of actions and events	AVERAGE
Behavior 38	Evaluate events with others to understand what happened	BELOW AVERAGE

18

Additional Development Recommendations

- Begin with brief, focused reflection sessions at the end of each day or week. Even spending a few minutes can help develop this habit and gradually build your reflective practice.

- Ask colleagues or mentors to provide feedback on your performance. Use this input as a basis for your reflection to identify areas for growth and improvement.

- Keep a simple log of key learnings from your experiences. Writing down insights can reinforce the habit of reflecting and make it easier to track your progress over time.

- Leverage tools like reflection apps or journals designed to facilitate the reflective process. These resources can provide structure and support as you develop your reflective skills.

- Establish clear, achievable goals for your reflection practice. Start with small, specific goals, and gradually increase the complexity as you become more comfortable with the process.

BB

Summary Scores

Summary Scores

Your Highest Dimension Scores

1	90	Collaborating	ABOVE AVERAGE
2	80	Flexibility	ABOVE AVERAGE
3	80	Information Gathering	ABOVE AVERAGE

Your Lowest Dimension Scores

1	7	Performance Risk Taking	BELOW AVERAGE
2	17	Interpersonal Risk Taking	BELOW AVERAGE
3	18	Reflecting	BELOW AVERAGE

Your Highest Behavior Scores

1	Collaborating	Collaborate with other parts of the organization	ABOVE AVERAGE
2	Collaborating	Work with colleagues from different backgrounds	ABOVE AVERAGE
3	Flexibility	Propose innovative solutions	ABOVE AVERAGE
4	Collaborating	Leverage skills, knowledge, and talent of others	ABOVE AVERAGE
5	Flexibility	Articulate different ideas/perspectives	ABOVE AVERAGE

Your Lowest Behavior Scores

1	Performance Risk Taking	Embrace work that is risky	BELOW AVERAGE
2	Performance Risk Taking	Take on challenging roles	BELOW AVERAGE
3	Performance Risk Taking	Engage in ambiguous tasks	BELOW AVERAGE
4	Performance Risk Taking	Volunteer for projects that involve the possibility of failure	BELOW AVERAGE
5	Interpersonal Risk Taking	Challenge other's ideas that are shared by many	BELOW AVERAGE

BB

Your Action Plan

Strengths to Leverage

1 _____

_____

_____

_____

2 _____

_____

_____

_____

Strategies for Doing So

1 _____

_____

_____

_____

2 _____

_____

_____

_____

Opportunities to Improve

1 _____

_____

_____

_____

2 _____

_____

_____

_____

Strategies for Doing So

1 _____

_____

_____

_____

2 _____

_____

_____

_____

ƎB

SECTION II

CHAPTER 5

FLEXIBILITY

FLEXIBILITY: Being open to new ideas and proposing new solutions

What follows is an example of *Flexibility* from *Presidents and Their Generals: An American History of Command in War* by Matthew Moten (2014). In this section, John Fitzgerald Kennedy has assumed the presidency and inherits some issues from his predecessor, Dwight D. Eisenhower, which he must address.

> Eisenhower broke diplomatic relations with Castro's communist regime, leaving Kennedy as one adviser put it, holding "a grenade with the pin pulled." Ike's CIA had been planning an invasion of Cuba and training anti-Castro Cuban expatriates for the task. . . . Although the Joint Chiefs had analyzed the CIA's planning and found it slipshod, they muted their criticism. . . . On April 17, 1961, less than two months into Kennedy's term, thirteen hundred Cuban exiles landed in the Bay of Pigs and found themselves surrounded by fifteen times as many Castro Forces.
>
> The debacle humiliated the young president, who took personal responsibility and then fired the top two men in the CIA. . . . He felt that both the CIA and the JCS had tried to manipulate him to take an unwise military action, and vowed never again to be "overawed by professional military advice." . . .
>
> Soon after the Bay of Pigs debacle Kennedy called on Maxwell Taylor to investigate the failed operations. Taylor chaired a group whose final report sprayed blame around the government, from the CIA to the JCS to the NSC.
>
> " . . . The president took the [Taylor] memo and "rushed off to the Pentagon" to talk with the joint chiefs. . . . JFK told the skeptical group that he wanted their advice to "come to him directly and unfiltered." He thought of them, he said, "as more than military specialists." . . . Their advice "could not and should not be purely military," as political, economic and

other factors always impinged on a national security decision. . . . Shortly thereafter, Kennedy recalled Taylor to active
duty as a four-star general and appointed him military representative to the president, an entirely new position . . . Taylor
became Kennedy's general. (pp. 278-280)

In this example, Kennedy demonstrates an openness to new ideas
from Eisenhower, the joint chiefs and Maxwell Taylor. He ultimately creates a new role for Taylor that allows Taylor to best support Kennedy as
president.

What follows are three two-part scenarios involving different people in organizations. They are either individual contributors, managers or
senior managers. In the first part of each scenario, the person is faced with
a work situation that involves an unresolved issue. In the individual contributor example, the *Burke Learning Agility Inventory Self-Assessment*
results for the person are provided so you can see how the information
can be used to encourage learning agility. The last two scenarios also are in
two parts and incorporate *Burke Learning Agility Self-Assessment* results,
but the *Burke Learning Agility Self-Assessment* profile is not shown. Each
description of a scenario includes a missed opportunity to address a *Burke
Learning Agility Inventory Self-Assessment* dimension, and an example
that provides developmental activities to address it.

INDIVIDUAL CONTRIBUTOR

- Missed Opportunity to Address *Flexibility*

  Mary has been the head of accounts receivable for 10 years. The
  company has a paper-based accounting system and invoices are all
  sent at once at the end of the month. There is a plan in place to
  automate this system by the end of the year.

  Dwayne is responsible for accounts payable. He is in his early
  20s and very tech-savvy. He volunteered a year ago to automate
  accounts payable. Dwayne is seen as having the potential to become
  a CFO. After he finished automating his area, he volunteered to
  participate in a few task forces. With time to spare in his schedule,

he offers to help Mary get a head start on her automation, but she is not interested.

Mary attends a finance group off-site meeting, takes the *Burke Learning Agility Self-Assessment* and receives her profile. Given the situation described previously, what would be your advice to Mary on how to incorporate what she learned from the *Burke Learning Agility Self-Assessment* to improve her job situation?

FLEXIBILITY

Being open to new ideas and proposing new solutions.

Mary's Flexibility Score: 30

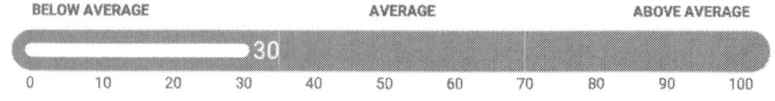

BELOW AVERAGE			AVERAGE				ABOVE AVERAGE	
0	10	20	30	40	50	60	70	80	90	100

30

			Norm Group
Behavior 1	Propose innovative solutions		BELOW AVERAGE
Behavior 2	Consider options before acting		AVERAGE
Behavior 3	Switch between different jobs/tasks		AVERAGE
Behavior 4	Find common themes among opposing points of view		BELOW AVERAGE
Behavior 5	Articulate different ideas/perspectives		BELOW AVERAGE

- Developmental activities to address *Burke Learning Agility Inventory Self-Assessment* weakness

One subject that the finance group always includes in its annual off-site meeting is professional development, and this year the professional development discussion includes the *Burke Learning*

Agility Self-Assessment. Mary's lowest score on the assessment concerns *Flexibility.* The next day in her one-on-one meeting with her boss, he asks Mary about her *Burke Learning Agility Self-Assessment* results. She shows her boss the feedback report. They both are interested in discussing her *Flexibility* score. The boss asks Mary if she thinks it is accurate. She thinks about it for a few seconds and nods her head "yes." He asks if this is something she wants to work on. Mary says she is willing to listen to the ideas her boss has but is concerned that they'll mean more work for her. Mary and her boss talk about whether to ask Dwayne to spend time in her area and make suggestions of things she can do to prepare for the coming automation. They agree that Mary must agree to all changes, and that Mary, her boss and Dwayne will meet monthly to review the project's progress. They agree that the automation could be accelerated to September, which would allow Mary to take off for two weeks in December to spend time with her son in London.

Here are two more scenarios, this time for a manager and senior manager. In the example involving two managers, only one person uses the *Burke Learning Agility Inventory* to address a stalemate at work. In the second example involving a senior manager, the *Burke Learning Agility Inventory* feedback was known and was used to improve the situation.

MANAGER

- Missed Opportunity to Address *Flexibility*

Josh is the manager of the budgeting group, and his coworker Rachel is the manager of the organizational effectiveness group. Rachel has been working with the head of sales to better differentiate pay for the company's high performers. For several years, the company had scheduled all salary increases at one time, on January 1 of each year. However, some people think it would be better for salary changes to be made on the anniversary of an employee's date of hire. This would not cost the company additional money, but would allow the head of sales to award bigger salary increases to his best performers. Josh does not like the suggestion, and argues that the company should stay with the schedule it has always used. He says that if he makes an exception for sales, he may have to make exceptions for other departments, which will add to his already heavy workload.

- Developmental Activities to Address *Burke Learning Agility Self-Assessment* Weakness

Josh and Rachel attend the annual manager's off-site meeting in Palm Springs. One of the topics covered at the meeting is learning agility. They both receive the feedback report on the *Burke Learning Agility Self-Assessment* that they took before the meeting. Josh's lowest score is in the area of *Flexibility*. Rachel scores very high in this area.

At the meeting, the attendees are broken into two groups. As luck would have it, Josh and Rachel are paired together. The facilitator asks everyone to write about one successful and one unsuccessful situation they have experienced at work and to ask themselves if using a particular learning agility dimension might have made a difference. Josh chooses this stalemate with Rachel and the sales organization as his unsuccessful situation. He doesn't know what learning agility dimension might make a difference in the outcome of this situation. Rachel suggests *Flexibility*.

By the time of the meeting, Rachel has completed additional work on this issue. She has determined that the biggest challenge is in setting up the alternative pay system. Once in place, no additional work will be required. She has calculated what the additional setup time might take in terms of hours and dollars, and then added 50% to her estimate. She persuades the head of sales to agree to pick up this additional cost in either overtime or a temporary person. When the facilitator asks the group for comments at the end of the session, Josh announces that the company will be implementing the sales project and it will help him improve his *Flexibility* score.

SENIOR MANAGER

- Missed Opportunity to Address *Flexibility*

Brenda, the CEO of a U.S.-based technology company, has recently completed the acquisition of a U.K.-based company of about equal size. The acquisition will provide the new company with additional products and services and a U.K. customer base. With the acquisition complete, the two companies must be integrated. Brenda assumes her team will take the lead on all the sub-teams. Her company, ABC Corp., has done several prior integrations in China. Brenda is confident that the integration will go smoothly, especially since everyone involved speaks the same language. The CEO of the acquired company, ACME, expects that leadership roles will be shared more equally.

- Developmental Activities to Address *Burke Learning Agility Inventory Self-Assessment* weakness

ACME has been through a previous acquisition attempt that failed miserably. As a result, the organization's leaders hire a consultant to lead some post-acquisition cross-cultural training sessions. One of the tools the consultant uses is the *Burke Learning Agility Self-Assessment*. Brenda's assessment shows that her lowest *Burke Learning Agility Self-Assessment* score is in the area of *Flexibility*. She is asked to write about a time when she was successful in her current role and another where she was unsuccessful. For her unsuccessful experience, Brenda tells about a specific time that she was resistant to others' ideas. Knowing this about herself, Brenda asks the consultant to lead a special session for her and her team to look at the issue of *Flexibility*. With the consultant's help, Brenda's team gives her several examples where her lack of *Flexibility* has been problematic. Brenda thanks her team for their candor. She also asks the consultant if he would facilitate a meeting with her and the CEO of ACME. The purpose of the meeting will be to revisit the integration discussion and equally divide the roles among the teams. They also create a mechanism for the two senior leaders to talk any time they or the teams get stuck.

CHAPTER 6

SPEED

SPEED: Acting on ideas quickly so that those not working are discarded and other possibilities are accelerated

This chapter begins with an example of both *Speed* and *Experimenting* from David McCullough's book, *The Wright Brothers* (2015). In this part of the story, the Wright brothers are back at Kitty Hawk, NC, where they are conducting several experiments using curvature dimension of the wing that they acquired from another aviator, Otto Lilienthal. The *Speed* part of this example is that the Wrights pretty quickly determine that the ratio they were given and have been using is not working. They stop their experiments, hurriedly make adjustments and continue their trials. The person named Katharine mentioned in this passage is their sister.

> Wilbur went again. And again. Several times the same experiment was repeated and with the same result.
>
> "The adjustments of the machine are way off," Orville explained to Katharine. The curvature, or camber, of the wings from the leading edges to the rear was too great and had to be changed. . . . What was so troubling was that the ratio they had gone by was exactly what Lilienthal had recommended, about 1 to 12, whereas for their glider of the year before, Machine No. 1, the brothers had used a ratio of 1 to 22.
>
> They stopped gliding for several days to rebuild— flatten—the wings back to a camber close to what it had been in 1900, and with fine results.
>
> . . . Octave Chanute left Kitty Hawk two days later, convinced the Wrights had made more progress and with a larger glider than anyone thus far, and urged them to keep on with their work. (pp. 61-63)

In this example, Wilbur repeats his experiment several times, checking and making adjustments as necessary. He and his brother act quickly to try to solve their problem, make the required changes, and then accelerate their actions once they determine the cause of the problem. In doing so, they demonstrate *Speed*.

To further illustrate *Speed* as a dimension of learning agility, here are three work scenarios involving different people in hypothetical organizations. As in the previous chapter, the scenarios involve individual contributors, managers and senior managers.

The first part of each scenario describes the person's response to an unresolved issue at work. In the individual contributor example, you can review the person's *Burke Learning Agility Inventory Self-Assessment* results and see how the data can be used to encourage learning agility. The last two scenarios also are in two parts and incorporate *Burke Learning Agility Self-Assessment* results without a profile. Each includes a missed opportunity to address a *Burke Learning Agility Inventory Self-Assessment* dimension, as well as developmental activities that could strengthen it.

INDIVIDUAL CONTRIBUTOR

- Missed Opportunity to Address *Speed*

  Marta is a very meticulous and well-regarded lab technician. She has been working for months on a series of experiments to isolate a critical variable by eliminating other variables. Each day and week that go by are costing her company thousands of dollars. Some of Marta's peers think that many of her trials are unnecessary.

  Marta attends a class at work and receives the following *Burke Learning Agility Self-Assessment* profile during the session. Given the situation described here, what would your advice be to Marta on how to incorporate what she learned from the *Burke Learning Agility Self-Assessment* to improve her situation on the job?

SPEED

Acting on ideas quickly so that those not working
are discarded and other possibilities are accelerated.

Marta's Speed Score: 30

BELOW AVERAGE		AVERAGE		ABOVE AVERAGE

30

0	10	20	30	40	50	60	70	80	90	100

30

		Norm Group
Behavior 6	Quickly develop solutions	AVERAGE
Behavior 7	Get up to speed in new projects/tasks	AVERAGE
Behavior 8	Readily grasp new ideas/concepts	BELOW AVERAGE
Behavior 9	Acquire new skills and knowledge rapidly	BELOW AVERAGE
Behavior 10	React well to unexpected problems	BELOW AVERAGE

- Developmental Activities to Address *Burke Learning Agility Inventory Self-Assessment* Weakness

Marta and her supervisor sit down and review all the data she has collected on her current project. They determine that she is looking at 10 different variables. Up to this point, she has been conducting 10 separate experiments, one for each variable. There is an element that is common to five of the 10 variables. If this element is identified in an experiment with one variable, it is not necessary to conduct experiments with the other four. This change in approach will allow Marta to reduce the number of experiments she conducts by 70%. This will allow Marta to do deeper research in the areas where this overarching element appears, and to have those results in about 20% less time. Marta and her supervisor agree on a new accelerated research plan and to meet in one month to review how it is working.

MANAGER

- Missed Opportunity to Address *Speed*

Keba is the division manager in a sales organization and has five district managers (DMs) who report to him. His organization is introducing several new products, and his division is behind in attaining its sales quota for the year. Keba attends a division manager's meeting where he completes and receives feedback on the *Burke Learning Agility Self-Assessment*. His lowest score on the test is in the area of *Speed*. Keba shares the results of his *Burke Learning Agility Self-Assessment* with the instructor. Keba talks about the fact that his division is behind on its plan. The two discuss how he might address this issue in his upcoming district manager meeting.

- Developmental Activities to Address *Burke Learning Agility Self-Assessment* Weakness

Keba calls a meeting of his DMs. He tells the group that the purpose of the meeting is to look at sales results year-to-date and see if they can find opportunities to improve their results in the next quarter. He gives each DM a printout that shows sales by account, product and month. In particular, he wants to look at new product sales. The DMs look at the number of calls made, follow-up rates and closed sales. It appears that some of the DMs are spending too much time on prospects and not enough time on growing business from existing accounts. Each DM creates a list of A-, B- and C-level accounts and a different call frequency for each. They agree to spend 20% of their time on closing new product sales, and that they will not make more than three calls on "no buy" accounts. The DMs agree to meet monthly to review progress with the new approach.

SENIOR MANAGER

- Missed Opportunity to Address *Speed*

Pat is the president of a company in an industry that's going through rapid consolidation. This is due to a legislative change that will go into effect at the end of the year that will make it impossible for many of the company's competitors to continue to exist. There is a "fire sale" opportunity for Pat to acquire some of these organizations, but each deal must be negotiated individually. Pat's legal team has told him that each negotiation is unique and must start from scratch. The company cannot quickly hire additional staff because very few people have deep knowledge of the industry in which the company works. Time is running out and several opportunities will be left on the table.

Pat is on a conference board council with presidents of several peer companies. At the group's last meeting, one of the topics was learning agility. The consultant facilitating the meeting administered and gave the council members feedback on the *Burke Learning Agility Inventory Self-Assessment*. Pat learned his lowest score was in the area of *Speed*. He had been working on a couple of projects to strengthen this area, so when this current issue arose, he saw it as another opportunity to work on *Speed*.

- Developmental Activities to Address *Burke Learning Agility Inventory Self-Assessment* Weakness

Pat meets with his head of organizational development and asks him to figure out a way to get the legal department to work differently so the company can close all viable deals by yearend. After a series of meetings with the legal team involved on this project, there is acceptance of a common set of templates that can be used on every potential acquisition. Each deal can be negotiated and closed in a week's time versus the one to two months it would have taken previously. It is understood that there may be a series of small revisions that will need to be made to each deal in January, but this is a trade-off to be able to take advantage of opportunities that are only available this year.

CHAPTER 7

EXPERIMENTING

EXPERIMENTING: Trying out new behaviors (approaches, ideas) to determine what is effective

In this chapter, we again turn to *The Wright Brothers* by David McCullough (2015) for examples of both *Speed* and *Experimenting*. As in the previous chapter, this part of the story is centered on the Wrights and their experiments using the curvature dimension of the wing, measurements they acquired from aviator Otto Lilienthal. Once the Wright brothers realize the measurements they received and have been using are inaccurate, they quickly stop the experiments, make adjustments, and continue their trials.

> But no sooner was the machine up than it nosed straight into the ground . . . Wilbur, it seemed, had positioned himself too far forward. In a second try, having shifted back a bit, he did no better. Finally, after several more failed attempts, he moved back nearly a foot from where he started and sailed off more than 100 yards.
>
> To all present but Wilbur and Orville, this flight seemed a huge success. To the brothers, it was disappointing. . . . Something was "radically wrong."
>
> In a glide later the same day, the machine kept rising higher . . . till it lost all headway, exactly "the fix" that plunged Otto Lilienthal to his death. Responding to a shout from Orville, Wilbur turned the rudder to its full extent and only then did the glider settle slowly to the ground, . . . landing with no damage or injury.
>
> Wilbur went again. And again. Several times the same experience was repeated and with the same result. . . .
>
> "The adjustments of the machine are way off," Orville explained to Katharine. The curvature, or "camber," of the wings . . . was too great and had to be changed. . . . [The] ratio they had gone by was what Lilienthal had recommended . . . 1 to 12 . . . [F]or their glider the year before . . . the brothers had used a ratio of 1 to 22. (p. 61)

In this example, the Wrights demonstrate *Experimenting* by being willing to try different approaches and ideas when the first ratio fails to give them the results they want.

Now let's take this description of *Experimenting* and apply it to the present-day work world, again using scenarios involving an individual contributor, manager or senior manager. In the first part of each scenario, the person faces an unresolved issue at work. In the individual contributor example, you can review the person's *Burke Learning Agility Self-Assessment* report and see how it can be used to encourage learning agility. The last two scenarios also are in two parts and incorporate *Burke Learning Agility Self-Assessment* results, but without the profile chart. Each description includes a missed opportunity to address a *Burke Learning Agility Self-Assessment* dimension, as well as developmental activities to address it.

INDIVIDUAL CONTRIBUTOR

- Missed Opportunity to Address *Experimenting*

    Arturo is an accountant at a high-tech firm that has been in business for 10 years. Arturo has been with the company and in his current role for two years, and was trained for his job by the woman who started the department. He and everyone in accounting accepts that the process they were taught for consolidating and reporting information works excellently. However, Arturo also knows that his customers often have difficulty interpreting the information from his department, as the format that they use for all lines of business doesn't work as well in some of the company's new lines. Arturo sees his boss as his primary customer and as long as she is happy with what he is providing, he is not inclined to make changes.

    Arturo attends the company's new culture class, and during the session completes and receives the *Burke Learning Agility Self-Assessment* profile and report. Given the scenario previously described and this profile, what advice would you give Arturo about incorporating what he learned from the *Burke Learning Agility Self-Assessment* to improve his situation on the job?

EXPERIMENTING

Trying out new behaviors (i.e., approaches, ideas) to determine what is effective.

Arturo's Experimenting Score: 20

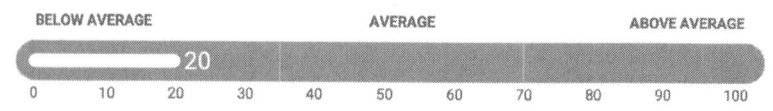

BELOW AVERAGE	AVERAGE	ABOVE AVERAGE

| | 0 | 10 | 20 | 30 | 40 | 50 | 60 | 70 | 80 | 90 | 100 |

Norm Group

Behavior 11	Evaluate new ways of solving problems		BELOW AVERAGE
Behavior 12	Experiment with unproven ideas		BELOW AVERAGE
Behavior 13	Try different approaches		BELOW AVERAGE
Behavior 14	Learn by trial and error		BELOW AVERAGE

20

- Developmental Activities to Address *Burke Learning Agility Inventory Self-Assessment* Weakness

Arturo confirms that *Experimenting* is not something he is inclined to do on the job. He and his boss sit down and discuss Arturo's *Burke Learning Agility Inventory Self-Assessment*. She gives him permission to go talk to a customer, who receives reports from his department. She and Arturo agree that he will go and ask the customer to identify three things that should be added to the report. Arturo agrees to come back and review the customer's "wants" with his boss before changing the report. If Arturo and his boss are in agreement about the change, then he will go ahead and make it. They also agree that Arturo and his boss will sit down with the same customer in three months to ask how the changes are working. Arturo and his boss will also sit down together and discuss how his *Experimenting* went, including what went well and what he might do differently the next time. Before the conversation is over, Arturo and his supervisor will find another opportunity for Arturo to use *Experimenting* at work.

What follows next are scenarios for a manager and senior manager. In the first example in each scenario, a situation occurred but the people involved did not have information from the *Burke Learning Agility Inventory Self-Assessment*. In the second part of the scenarios, the *Burke Learning Agility Inventory Self-Assessment* feedback was known and was used to improve the situation.

MANAGER

- Missed Opportunity to Address *Experimenting*

  Clovis is the manager of an engineering group that puts together bid packages for potential projects. The company he works for has grown by 50% in the last five years. Three years ago, Clovis's group did attempt to redesign the way it prepares bids, but the effort was very unsuccessful. As the business has grown, the engineering group has added more staff to try to keep up.

- Developmental Activities to Address *Burke Learning Agility Self-Assessment* Weakness

  In preparation to attend a first-line supervisor training session, Clovis takes the *Burke Learning Agility Self-Assessment*. In reviewing his *Burke Learning Agility Self-Assessment* report, Clovis is not really surprised that his lowest learning agility dimension is *Experimenting*. When asked about an opportunity where he could experiment in his current job, he brings up improving the bid preparation process. Clovis agrees to have his team meet with the engineering department to ask how they would change the bid process to make it more useful and effective. Clovis's boss empowers him to create three separate experiments to determine whether his team agrees with what the engineering department sees as important. They review the results with the department supervisor after the experiment. Clovis and his boss sit down and talk about how the trials associated with the changes have been helpful, as well as what could be improved. Before Clovis leaves the session, he needs to determine what three to five new changes he is going to make by the end of 2024.

SENIOR MANAGER

• Missed Opportunity to Address *Experimenting*

Naomi is the vice president of human resources for a 1,000-person manufacturing organization. The company has had the same recruiting process for 10 years. Naomi thinks turnover at the company is above average for its geographic area and industry, but has no data to support whether she's right. At the company, human resources is responsible for providing candidates for open positions, and then the leaders of each department decide who they want to hire. Naomi knows the process could be improved, but feels she doesn't have the time to make changes when no one is complaining.

• Developmental Activities to Address *Burke Learning Agility Inventory Self-Assessment* Weakness

Naomi attends a management conference that includes feedback on the *Burke Learning Agility Self-Assessment*, which she and her colleagues took in advance. The president of Naomi's division asks to meet with her to discuss some involuntary turnover that is making it difficult to complete an important project. Naomi happens to have her *Burke Learning Agility Inventory Self-Assessment* results with her and shares that her lowest score is in the area of *Experimenting*. Naomi and her boss agree that the recruiting process needs to be improved, and discuss a few ideas. Naomi agrees to get feedback from her department and her customers, and to meet with the president in two weeks to review the top three changes her department will make to address the issue of involuntary turnover. The president assures her that she will tell Naomi's customers in the company that this change is important to the organization. Naomi gets the feedback, meets with her boss, and implements the three experiments. Three months later, she reviews the results with the president, her team, and her customers within the company. Naomi and the president also talk about what went well with these experiments and what she can do better next time. They identify the next round of experiments and set due dates.

CHAPTER 8

PERFORMANCE RISK TAKING

PERFORMANCE RISK TAKING: Seeking new activities (tasks, assignments, roles) to determine what is effective

David McCullough's book *The Wright Brothers* (2015) offers several examples of *Performance Risk Taking*. In this excerpt, it is 1901 and the Wright brothers' reputation is growing. One of the top experts in this burgeoning field, Octave Chanute, asks Wilbur to speak at an important professional meeting. The "Katharine" mentioned below is the Wrights' sister.

> . . . [In] August came an invitation from Octave Chanute for Wilbur to address the Western Society of Engineers in Chicago on the subject of gliding experiments. It was his first request to speak in public, and he was extremely reluctant to accept, feeling the date set, September 18, left too little time to prepare anything of substance. But Katharine "nagged" him into going. That Wilbur might prove a poor speaker seems never to have entered her thoughts.

> . . . Octave Chanute had written to inquire whether he would mind if the meeting of the society was designated "Ladies Night." . . . . "I will already be as badly scared as it is possible for a man to be." Asked by Katharine and Orville whether his talk would be scientific or witty, he said, "Pathetic."

> . . . The speech Wilbur delivered—modestly titled "Some Aeronautical Experiments"—would be quoted again and again for years to come. Published first in the society's journal, it appeared in . . . *The Engineering Magazine, Scientific American,* the magazine, Flying, and the *Annual Report of the Smithsonian Institution.* In the words of . . . [an] aeronautics specialist at the Library of Congress, the speech was "the Book of Genesis of the twentieth-century Bible of Aeronautics." (pp. 66-67)

The performance risk taken by Wilbur Wright was to deliver a presentation at an important meeting, a "risk" for someone who had no public speaking experience.

What follows next are three two-part scenarios involving different people in organizations: individual contributors, managers or senior managers. In the first part of each scenario, the person is faced with a work situation that involves an unresolved issue. In the individual contributor example, the *Burke Learning Agility Inventory Self-Assessment* results for the person are provided so you can see how the information can be used to encourage learning agility. The last two scenarios are also in two parts and incorporate *Burke Learning Agility Self-Assessment* results, but the profile is not shown. Each description includes a missed opportunity to address a *Burke Learning Agility Self-Assessment* dimension and an example of developmental activities for the individual.

INDIVIDUAL CONTRIBUTOR

- Missed Opportunity to Address *Performance Risk Taking*

Diego is a line operator on a production line. He is seen as one of the best performers in his area. His company has been around for 50 years and has been very successful, but big changes are coming for Diego. Senior management has determined through analysis that Diego's plant and its production lines need to either be modernized or closed and replaced with a new facility. The company ultimately decides to do a modernization. At the same time, Diego is feeling restless and unchallenged in his current role. He knows his next step up is supervision, but he doesn't know if he will enjoy managing people.

Diego attends a training day related to the plant modernization and receives his *Burke Learning Agility Inventory Self-Assessment* profile during the session. Given the situation described here, what advice would you give Diego on how he can improve his situation using information learned from the *Burke Learning Agility Self-Assessment?*

PERFORMANCE RISK TAKING

Seeking new activities (i.e., tasks, assignments, roles)
that provide opportunities to be challenged.

Diego's Performance Risk Taking Score: 25

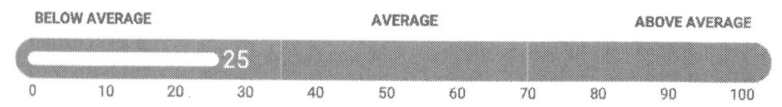

		Norm Group
Behavior 15	Take on challenging roles	AVERAGE
Behavior 16	Engage in ambiguous tasks	BELOW AVERAGE
Behavior 17	Embrace work that is risky	BELOW AVERAGE
Behavior 18	Volunteer for projects that involve the possibility of failure	BELOW AVERAGE

25

- Developmental Activities to Address *Burke Learning Agility Self-Assessment* Weakness

There were a lot of activities going on in the plant related to its modernization. The production team has a training day built into its schedule every two weeks. The most recent session focused on learning agility, since it was going to be a big part of the modernization, and members of the team completed and received feedback on the *Burke Learning Agility Inventory Self-Assessment*. Diego's lowest score came back in the area of *Performance Risk Taking*. He and his supervisor talk about the results, along with Diego's restlessness, and create a plan for him that takes advantage of the changes that are occurring. Because production goals still need to be met while the plant is modernized, some workers will be asked to tackle two jobs at the same time. They will be responsible for their regular duties while taking on the additional task of setting up and starting production on the new lines. Temporary team leads will oversee this start-up process.

Diego jumps at the opportunity to work as a temporary team lead. He and his supervisor agree that they will meet weekly during the set-up and start-up process to discuss what is working and not working for him as a team lead. This will help Diego decide if he wants to pursue a permanent supervisory position with the company.

The next two scenarios are for a manager and a senior manager. Both examples involve conflicts at work, and how feedback from the *Burke Learning Agility Self-Assessment* can be used to improve the outcomes.

MANAGER

- Missed Opportunity to Address *Performance Risk Taking*

  Francesca is a manager of her company's cloud services group, a growing part of the business. The company's turnover, both voluntary and non-voluntary, has been about 20% for the last year. Francesca feels like her department is a revolving door, and that a big portion of her time is spent on talent acquisition. She attended the company's interviewing course nine months ago to build on her skills, and feels like she does a good job of assessing people's technical skills. She suspects that much of the company's turnover has to do with "cultural fit" issues and the inability of some of her new hires to get along with their teams.

- Developmental Activities to Address *Burke Learning Agility Inventory Self-Assessment* Weakness

  Francesca brings this issue up in a meeting she has with her boss, Leon. Leon suggests that Francesca go to HR and ask to review her *Burke Learning Agility Self-Assessment* report. She learns that her lowest score is in the area of *Performance Risk Taking*. She and Leon meet again and talk about Francesca's staffing issue, using her *Burke Learning Agility Self-Assessment* as a reference. Leon reminds Francesca that he started in the company's corporate planning group for high-potential employees. This group does on-campus recruiting of MBA students. It uses a fairly rigorous structured interview and members of the group work in teams of two. The two interviewers debrief after each interview and compare ratings. If ratings differ by more than one point, the recruiters must present data from the candidate's examples that supports the rating.

Leon thinks he can get the corporate planning group to take Francesca along on a few of their weekend recruiting trips. He knows they will want to train her first, because she will be helping them to select candidates. Francesca comes back from the first trip a changed person, and is ready to make significant modifications to the selection process for the cloud services group. She can't wait for the second trip with corporate planning.

SENIOR MANAGER

- Missed Opportunity to Address *Performance Risk Taking*

Roland is the CEO of AMP, a $1.5 billion conglomerate. AMP has three roughly equal-sized businesses: financial services, logistics and manufacturing. Each of the businesses is headed by a president. Roland is 62 years old and plans to retire in three to five years. The head of AMP's logistics business is 64 years old, and has told Roland privately that he intends to retire in 12 to 18 months. Roland knows he quickly needs to find his new president of logistics, and also his own replacement. He thinks he may have an internal candidate for the logistics position, but not for his own role. The looming problem has Roland worried. Unsure of where to turn, he sets up a date to play golf and talk with his friend Brandan, who owns a recruiting firm.

- Developmental Activities to Address *Burke Learning Agility Inventory Self-Assessment* Weakness

After a round of golf that includes talking about Roland's concerns, Brandan asks Roland if he knows of the *Burke Learning Agility Self-Assessment*. Roland says no. Brandan suggests that Roland take it so the two of them can review Roland's results and discuss how to apply them. Brandan says that the *Burke Learning Agility Self-Assessment* may provide useful information about Roland that could be used during an external search for the company's next CEO. Roland completes the *Burke Learning Agility Inventory Self-Assessment* and finds that his lowest score is in the area of *Performance Risk Taking*. He knows this is accurate. He meets with Brandan and they discuss his *Burke Learning Agility Self-Assessment* results in the context of some senior personnel changes he needs to address.

They agree to hire a consulting firm to do an assessment for development of the presidents of the finance and manufacturing divisions. The firm will also assess the potential successor in logistics. All assessments will use a cognitive agility test, a personality inventory, the *Burke Learning Agility Inventory Self-Assessment* and a structured interview. At the same time, the company will give additional responsibilities to Roland's logistics employee who is seen as a high-potential candidate, a person who could one day be promoted to president of logistics. His responsibilities will be shifted every six months to expose and "test" him in areas he has not managed. If he does well, he will be appointed as president of logistics in 18 months, and the current president will retire.

As part of the succession process, the presidents of finance and manufacturing also will be assessed for their performance in their current roles. Those results will be compared against the job requirements of their current roles as presidents. The information gathered will include their strengths and development needs, and will be summarized in their individual development plans. They each will be given 18 months to address the issues in their development plans, and will be assigned a coach to help them with their progress.

After those18 months are over, the two presidents will trade roles, go through a similar process, and receive development plans for their new assignments. In this second round, they will be compared against the standard, or job requirements, of the new role they are assuming. They also will be told that at the end of three years, one of them will likely become the company's new CEO. To that end, their development plans will include several activities that allow Roland to think about each of them in the role of CEO. Roland also agrees to hire Brandan to monitor the market in case plans change and he needs to hire a president from outside the company to run one of AMP's three businesses on short notice.

CHAPTER 9

INTERPERSONAL RISK TAKING

INTERPERSONAL RISK TAKING: Discussing differences with others in ways that lead to learning and change

This passage comes from Doris Kearns Goodwin's book *Team of Rivals* (2012). In this excerpt, Abraham Lincoln is trying to gain the necessary support in Congress to pass the 13th Amendment, which would abolish slavery.

> He assigned two of his allies in the House to deliver the votes of two wavering members. . . . [T]hey asked how to proceed, he said, "I am the President of the United States, clothed with great power. The abolition of slavery by constitutional provision settles the fate, for all coming time, not only of the millions now in bondage, but of unborn millions to come—a measure of such importance that those two votes must be procured. I leave it to you to determine how it shall be done; . . . I expect you to procure those votes." It was clear to his emissaries that his power extended to plum assignments, pardons, campaign contributions, and government jobs for relatives and friends. . . . Democrat Moses F. Odell agreed to change his vote; when the session ended, he was given the lucrative post of navy agent in New York.
>
> . . . [I]t appeared that the amendment had fallen two or three votes short of the . . . two-thirds margin . . . Speaker Colfax . . . announce[d] the final tally. . . . "On the passage to amend the Constitution of the United States the ayes have 119, the noes 56 . . . . the Joint Resolution has passed." Without the five Democrats who . . . changed their votes, the amendment would have lost. (pp. 687-689)

In this example, the interpersonal risks were taken by Lincoln's two allies. They were told by Lincoln to do whatever it took—give out plum assignments, pardons or even jobs—to get two members to change their votes so that the legislation passed. The men were successful, and the 13th Amendment became law.

To further illustrate *Interpersonal Risk Taking* as a dimension of learning agility, here are three work scenarios involving different people in hypothetical organizations. As in the previous chapter, the scenarios involve individual contributors, managers and senior managers.

The first part of each scenario describes the person's response to an unresolved issue at work. In the individual contributor example, you can review the person's *Burke Learning Agility Self-Assessment* results and see how they can be used to encourage learning agility. The last two scenarios are also in two parts and incorporate *Burke Learning Agility Self-Assessment* results without a profile. Each includes a missed opportunity to address a *Burke Learning Agility Self-Assessment* dimension, as well as developmental activities for the person described.

INDIVIDUAL CONTRIBUTOR

- Missed Opportunity to Address *Interpersonal Risk Taking*

  Marla is a sales representative for Con Gen, a global pharmaceutical company. She has 200 accounts that she calls on as a representative of the personal products unit, which is one of about 20 different business units within the company. Marla has a large territory, and she really needs to be organized to be able to call on all her accounts once a month. Some of the customers at one of her accounts, BiMore, have told her that they don't understand why they are called on by different salespeople from Con Gen's many business units. At her previous employer, Marla represented all of her company's products to each of her customers. Con Gen hired her away from that employer about a year ago with a good salary increase. Since joining Con Gen, Marla has heard that the company may centralize and integrate its various systems, but she's not sure how long she can wait. She is frustrated by efforts she sees as duplicative and inefficient.

  Marla attends Con Gen's sales convention, where she completes the *Burke Learning Agility Inventory Self-Assessment*. Her profile follows. What advice would you give Marla to help her apply what she learned from the *Burke Learning Agility Inventory Self-Assessment* to improve her situation with Con Gen and her customers at BiMore?

INTERPERSONAL RISK TAKING

Confronting differences with others in ways that lead to learning and change.

Marla's Interpersonal Risk Taking Score: 25

BELOW AVERAGE	AVERAGE	ABOVE AVERAGE

25

| 0 | 10 | 20 | 30 | 40 | 50 | 60 | 70 | 80 | 90 | 100 |

Norm Group

				Norm Group
25	Behavior 19	Bring up tough issues with others		BELOW AVERAGE
	Behavior 20	Ask others for help		BELOW AVERAGE
	Behavior 21	Discuss mistakes with others		AVERAGE
	Behavior 22	Challenge other's ideas that are shared by many		BELOW AVERAGE

- Developmental Activities to Address *Burke Learning Agility Self-Assessment* Weakness

Marla's lowest score on the *Burke Learning Agility Self-Assessment* is in the area of *Interpersonal Risk Taking.* She scores higher on *Collaborating,* but it is still one of her lowest scores. The tables at which people are sitting during the session are arranged by Con Gen customers to create synergy for discussions among the sales team. Her table is the BiMore table.

Marla's district manager is facilitating the discussion at her table. Marla shares with the group that her lowest scores are *Interpersonal Risk Taking,* followed by *Collaborating.* She sees this as an opportunity to start to work on *Interpersonal Risk Taking* by *Collaborating* with her peers. She tells the people at her table that she is frustrated and feels like she can't keep her customers happy because Con Gen's system and structure are working against her. This gets an immediate sympathetic response from her peers. The district manager is surprised by the comments. He appoints Marla as head of a task force to address this issue. Immediately, five of her peers volunteer to participate.

Next are scenarios for a manager and a senior manager. In the first part of each example, the person described has not taken the *Burke Learning Agility Inventory Self-Assessment.* In the second part, *Burke Learning Agility Inventory Self-Assessment* feedback is known and used to improve the situation or conflict.

MANAGER

- Missed Opportunity to Address *Interpersonal Risk Taking*

Bank Technology Solutions (BTS) is a midsize technology company that provides software to the financial services industry, primarily banks. Due to consolidation in banking, business has been brisk for several years. Bank Technology Solutions' back office is growing, but nowhere near the growth occurring in the sales department. The vice president of sales asks the human resources department for help in creating a more rigorous selection process that he hopes will lead to better hiring decisions. HR creates the process, but many on the sales team are resistant to it. They feel that they will know good salespeople when they meet them. As a result, several key people on the team are just going through the motions with the new process. The lack of buy-in becomes apparent when several new hires fail to make their sales goals and turnover spikes in the department. The president of Bank

Technology Solutions asks the company's senior managers about the new sales selection system at a managers' meeting. With the heads of HR and sales glaring at each other, he calls a break in the meeting.

• Developmental Activities to Address *Burke Learning Agility Self-Assessment* Weakness

The head of HR hires an outside consulting firm to take the senior management team through a session on the *Burke Learning Agility Self-Assessment* background and its individual and group composites. A consultant from the firm also attends a senior management meeting to get a feel for how the group members interact with each other. Each member of the sales teams also takes the *Burke Learning Agility Self-Assessment* to provide composite data for the group. The results from the sales team show that the group is fast (*Speed*) but not very collaborative. The team as a whole also scored low on *Interpersonal Risk Taking*.

The group agrees that the outcome for the next day's session is to address why the new selection process is not being used, and how to monitor its use moving forward.

SENIOR MANAGER

• Missed Opportunity to Address *Interpersonal Risk Taking*

Wolfgang was the CEO of a U.S. beer company. A year ago, his company and its Japanese counterpart entered into a joint venture (JV) in Japan. During that time, the CEOs of the Japanese and U.S. companies met once in each country. These were largely symbolic meetings over meals, and were attended by several of each company's senior managers.

The JV had not been congealing as either side had hoped that it would, in large part because of interference by and resistance from the U.S. company. There were also cultural differences hampering the JV. In Japan, much business is done after hours and includes alcohol. It is culturally acceptable for a Japanese manager to tell his boss what he *really* thinks about something in these situations. The next day all is forgotten or rationalized because the manager had had too much to drink.

In one of the CEO dinner meetings in Japan, a senior Japanese department head in the JV shares his unedited frustrations from the last year with the U.S. CEO. As is the custom in his country, the Japanese department head has consumed a lot of the company's product and is not afraid to offer his recommendations of what needs to be fixed in the JV. The American CEO is not accustomed to this kind of candor, and tells his security guard to help the Japanese department head get home. Most people at the dinner do not know that anything has happened. By the next day, the Japanese department head has been removed from the JV and reassigned to the Japanese parent company.

- Developmental Activities to Address *Burke Learning Agility Inventory Self-Assessment* Weakness

After a full year of struggle, it is suggested that leaders of both companies could benefit from cultural awareness training. The initial training is done within each organization, and includes taking and getting feedback on the Sage, a cross cultural awareness test, and the *Burke Learning Agility Inventory Self-Assessment*. Participants receive feedback on their individual learning agility needs, and results are prepared for each group. *Flexibility* is an issue that is identified by the Sage across each company. In addition, both companies learn that their employees' lowest score for the *Burke Learning Agility Inventory Self-Assessment* is on *Interpersonal Risk Taking*. Both companies' teams talk about how they could have handled the ill-fated evening's events more effectively. This leads to both companies feeling that they have a better understanding of some of their cultural differences.

The two groups come together as one group and talk about what they can do to better communicate and anticipate such issues before they become crises. They also agree to meet once a year to monitor how things are progressing. In a joint session, the two CEOs encourage the JV employees to take risks in their performance and interpersonal interactions. Questions are encouraged during the joint CEO meeting and many are asked. One of the suggestions is to begin preparation for these JV meetings with the CEOs much earlier, involve more people, and work to socialize the norms and expectations for all participants in advance.

CHAPTER 10

COLLABORATING

COLLABORATING: Finding ways to work with others that generate unique opportunities for learning

This chapter on *Collaborating* begins with a different example from David McCullough's book *The Wright Brothers* (2015). Orville and Wilbur Wright are continuing to conduct trials of their glider, but this time they have some assistance from several colleagues of Octave Chanute, an aviation pioneer.

> As it happened, one of the two men Octave Chanute wished to join the brothers in their experiments had arrived just as the mosquitoes struck and shared in their miseries. He was Edward Huffaker of Chuckey City, Tennessee, a former employee of the Smithsonian Institution and author of a Smithsonian pamphlet, *On Soaring Flight*. Now a protégé of Chanute, he had brought with him a disassembled glider of his own design built at Chanute's expense . . .
>
> The second to join the group, young George Alexander Spratt from Coatesville, Pennsylvania, had little in the way of appropriate background for the work at hand . . . About all he could offer as a reason for his participation was that flying had been the dream of his life . . .
>
> . . . As tiresome as anything for the sons of Bishop Wright was to hear Huffaker go on about "character building," rather than hard work, being the great aim of life.
>
> Spratt, by contrast, helped every way he could and was excellent company. (pp. 59-60)

So in this example, the Wright Brothers found ways to collaborate with Huffaker and Spratt on their flying experiments. Each of them brought different capabilities and they all learned from each other in the process.

For more examples of *Collaborating* in action, here are three two-part scenarios involving different people in organizations—individual contributors, managers or senior managers. In the first part of each scenario, the person is faced with a work situation that involves an unresolved issue. In the individual contributor example, the *Burke Learning Agility Self-Assessment* results for the person are provided so you can see how it can be used to encourage learning agility.

The last two scenarios are also in two parts and incorporate *Burke Learning Agility Self-Assessment* results, but the profile is not shown. Each description includes a missed opportunity to address a *Burke Learning Agility Self-Assessment* dimension, and an example that provides developmental activities for the individual.

INDIVIDUAL CONTRIBUTOR

• Missed opportunity to Address *Collaborating*

Lars works as an international sports marketing specialist, a role that his company created three years ago. Lars handles the promotions for all the company's brands in every sports segment. He is located in London, but the company's headquarters are in Miami. When Lars started in this role, he attended some events in the U.S. that were sponsored by his company to better understand how things were done. He learned a lot, but now 100% of his time is devoted to planning and executing events and promotions. He feels isolated in his day-to-day work and disconnected from the team in Miami. When challenges arise on the job, he feels like he has no one to turn to for input or help.

Before attending a country manager meeting in London, Lars completes the *Burke Learning Agility Self-Assessment* and receives his feedback report. Based on the information here, how can he improve his work situation?

COLLABORATING

Lars' Collaborating Score: 20

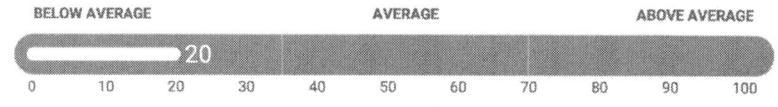

BELOW AVERAGE	AVERAGE	ABOVE AVERAGE

0   10   20   30   40   50   60   70   80   90   100

Norm Group

20

Behavior 23	Leverage skills, knowledge, and talent of others	BELOW AVERAGE
Behavior 24	Work with colleagues from different backgrounds	BELOW AVERAGE
Behavior 25	Collaborate with other parts of the organization	BELOW AVERAGE
Behavior 26	Ask stakeholders for their point of view	BELOW AVERAGE

- Developmental Activities to Address *Burke Learning Agility Self-Assessment* Weakness

Lars is not surprised that his lowest score on the *Burke Learning Agility Self-Assessment* is *Collaborating*, since he rarely has opportunities to work closely with the team in Miami. The head of international operations suggests that Lars reach out to Renaldo, the head of sports marketing in the United States. Lars meets with Renaldo, and they agree to do a best practices-sharing session at Renaldo's next sports marketing meeting. Renaldo also suggests that everyone bring a problem they are trying to solve and use the meeting as a place to brainstorm solutions. The meeting goes well, and the group asks to have this kind of meeting twice a year. The group also decides that the next meeting should include employees from field sales and national accounts.

Next are two scenarios, one for a manager and the other involving a senior manager. The first part of each scenario does not include any information from the *Burke Learning Agility Self-Assessment*. In the second part, the *Burke Learning Agility Self-Assessment* feedback is known and used to improve the situation at work.

MANAGER

- Missed Opportunity to Address *Collaborating*

  Julie and Caroline run the design and construction engineering groups, respectively, for a franchise fast food company. Design is a home-office role, while construction engineering is based wherever projects are located. Although Julie and Caroline get along when they are both in the office, they are rarely there at the same time. This is leading to problems for the company; in the last year, plans created in the design group could not be executed by the construction group, leading to delays and cost overruns. Neither Caroline nor Julie has taken the initiative to address the issue.

- Developmental Activities to Address *Burke Learning Agility Self-Assessment* Weakness

  Caroline and Julie both report to Al, the vice president of engineering. He recently took the *Burke Learning Agility Inventory Self-Assessment*, which the company is using with its executives. Al talks to Julie and Caroline, and then the company's internal organization development consultant, about using the *Burke Learning Agility Inventory Self-Assessment* as a tool to address the issue the two are having. Julie's lowest score is in the area of *Collaborating*. Caroline has an average score in *Collaborating*, but a lower score in the area of *Interpersonal Risk Taking*. The consultant asks Julie and Caroline if they think the scores are accurate, and they do. The consultant recommends that Julie and Caroline talk about how they might better collaborate, which leads them to try something new. For an upcoming project, Julie assigns the lead designer to Caroline for one month. She also identifies a second person in her group as a liaison that anyone from Caroline's group can go to when there is a problem. Julie and Caroline agree to hold a joint staff meeting in one month to talk to their teams about ways to collaborate. They also decide to do a "pulse" survey every three months to monitor whether the skill of *Collaborating* is increasing within their groups.

SENIOR MANAGER

- Missed Opportunity to Address *Collaborating*

Pat and Kevin are both senior managers at a $10 billion consumer products company. Pat is the president of the beverage subsidiary, while Kevin is the president of the much smaller snacks division.

Kevin and Pat are both members of the strategy committee, but outside that responsibility, have little interaction. Recently, the head of HR asked the members of the strategy committee to complete the *Burke Learning Agility Self-Assessment* so they would be familiar with the tool the company plans to use in its succession planning efforts. Nothing is done with the *Burke Learning Agility Self-Assessment* information other than to describe the dimensions and what they mean. This occurs during a strategy committee meeting.

- Developmental Activities to Address *Burke Learning Agility Self-Assessment* Weakness

After the strategy committee meeting, Ernesto, the head of HR, shares the *Burke Learning Agility Inventory Self-Assessment* profiles of the executive group with the company's CEO. Across all operations and positions, everyone's lowest score is *Collaborating*. The CEO meets with Pat and Kevin and tells them what he has learned from Ernesto based on *Burke Learning Agility Inventory*

Self-Assessment data. He asks Kevin and Pat to meet to discuss ways they can collaborate, and then share how they will learn from each other with members of the executive group at a future meeting. The CEO also offers Ernesto as a resource for their discussions. Kevin agrees to show Pat how to do some small-scale tests, and Pat says he'll look for ways that Kevin could scale some of his bigger products.

CHAPTER 11

INFORMATION GATHERING

INFORMATION GATHERING: Using various methods to remain current in one's area of expertise

At this point in David McCullough's book, *The Wright Brothers* (2015), it is the 1890s, a great period in American history for inventions and innovations. The town of Dayton, Ohio, where the Wright brothers lived, ranks the highest per capita in patents issued by the U.S. patent office. Wilbur Wright is becoming more and more interested in air travel, and is trying to read and learn as much as he can on the topic.

> In his letter to the Smithsonian, Wilbur made mention of his interest in birds. To achieve human flight, he had written, was "only a question of knowledge and skill in all acrobatic feats," and birds were "the most perfectly trained gymnasts in the world . . . specially well fitted for their work."

> Among the material the Smithsonian provided him was an English translation of a book titled *L'Empire de l'Air*, published in Paris in 1881. It had been written by a French farmer, poet, and student of flight, Louis Pierre Mouillard. Nothing Wilbur had yet read so affected him. He would long consider it "one of the most remarkable pieces of aeronautical literature" ever published. For Wilbur, flight had become a "cause," and Mouillard, one of the great "missionaries" of the cause . . . of human flight."

> At the start of his *Empire of the Air,* Mouillard gave fair warning that one could be entirely overtaken by the thought that the problem of flight could be solved by man. "When once this idea has invaded the brain, it possesses it exclusively." (p. 36)

In this example of *Information Gathering*, Wilbur reached out to the Smithsonian to acquire the most current knowledge available on birds and flight. He recognized that he needed to increase his knowledge to accomplish his goal—manned flight.

To further illustrate *Information Gathering*, this chapter ends with three scenarios, each involving an individual contributor, manager or senior manager who is facing a challenge at work. Each scenario is written in two parts—the first describes the challenge at work but offers no way to solve it; the second shows how the person uses the *Burke Learning Agility Self-Assessment* and information about his or her weakness in *Information Gathering* to improve in this area.

The example involving the individual contributor also includes profile information from the *Burke Learning Agility Self-Assessment*.

INDIVIDUAL CONTRIBUTOR

- Missed Opportunity to Address *Information Gathering*

Russ manages a regional office in rural Idaho that is part of a $200 million specialty products company. Russ came to the company as an administrative assistant, but was soon promoted to his current role. Because the office is small, with only a few employees, Russ is assigned many "collateral" duties, including safety, human resources, and information technology. Russ has not been trained in these areas, and does not always receive updates on policy changes affecting them. Because the office is in a remote location, he rarely is able to attend corporate meetings, even if his boss remembers to invite him. Russ feels like important safety and HR compliance issues are slipping through the cracks. His concerns prove to be warranted when his office receives a reprimand for missing an OSHA submission date.

Russ manages to get some time out of the office to attend an administrative update meeting his company is holding in Chicago. The agenda includes a session about the *Burke Learning Agility Inventory Self-Assessment*. After the session, Russ completes and receives feedback on the *Burke Learning Agility Inventory Self-Assessment*. A copy of his report follows. What would be your advice to Russ on how he can use the results of the *Burke Learning Agility Inventory Self-Assessment* to improve his work situation?

INFORMATION GATHERING

Russ' Information Gathering Score: 35

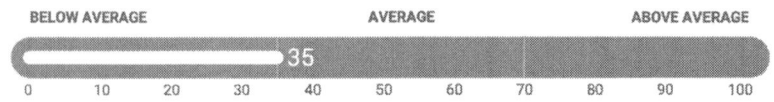

			Norm Group
Behavior 27	Seek new information on topics related to your own field		BELOW AVERAGE
Behavior 28	Update knowledge through training and education		AVERAGE
Behavior 29	Read books, journals, blogs, articles, etc. to stay informed		AVERAGE
Behavior 30	Collect data to increase knowledge and inform next steps		BELOW AVERAGE

- Developmental Activities to Address *Burke Learning Agility Self-Assessment* Weakness

Russ's lowest score on his *Burke Learning Agility Inventory Self-Assessment* profile is *Information Gathering.* He thinks his score is spot on. After returning to Idaho, Russ schedules a meeting with his boss to discuss what he learned in Chicago, including about the *Burke Learning Agility Inventory Self-Assessment.* Russ shares his *Burke Learning Agility Self-Assessment* results with his boss, and tells him how it helps explain some of the frustration he's been feeling at work. Russ doesn't want to let the office down by missing deadlines.

The boss asks Russ to develop a resource planning document, which should help him better manage the duties he handles outside his primary role. Since the biggest one of those is HR, Russ is encouraged and given approval to attend local meetings of the Society for Human Resource Management. Russ and his boss also agree to meet once a quarter to talk specifically about whether Russ is feeling up-to-date in the knowledge required to perform his collateral duties, and to discuss any connections or resources he has identified or needs to perform the collateral duties he has been assigned.

The next two scenarios are for a manager and a senior manager. In the first example in each scenario, information from the *Burke Learning Agility Inventory Self-Assessment* is not available to provide insight. In the second part, the *Burke Learning Agility Inventory Self-Assessment* feedback is known and used to improve the situation.

MANAGER

- Missed Opportunity to Address *Information Gathering*

  Leticia is the manager of the technical training function at Build Well Construction. Leticia has four direct reports, each of whom handles a specialty area of technical training within production. Representatives from Build Well Construction's vendors, who supply much of the company's equipment, often suggest changes to Leticia's direct reports that they should incorporate into their training sessions to improve efficiencies. However, this information is rarely shared with Leticia. In addition, Leticia and her direct reports only rarely attend continuing education sessions themselves or participate in e-learning classes. Leticia is hearing more negative comments about her group from the head of production, who regularly tells her about the cutting-edge training tools that are used at his wife's company.

- Developmental Activities to Address *Burke Learning Agility Inventory Self-Assessment* Weakness

  Leticia gets invited to a session of all the trainers in her company. Their session covers some new technologies the company has invested in, along with the *Burke Learning Agility Self-Assessment*. Leticia learns that her lowest dimension on the *Burke Learning Agility Self-Assessment* is on *Information Gathering*. She thinks about the last conversation she had with the head of production and the comments he made about technical training at his wife's company.

Leticia decides to share her *Burke Learning Agility Self-Assessment* results with her boss. Her boss agrees with Leticia's conclusion that while her group's training is technically sound, the delivery methods are not engaging. Leticia is prepared with a list of seminars she would like to attend with her four direct reports. She also wants to subscribe to a few journals, and suggests that any information her direct reports read on a relevant topic or learn in a class should be formally shared with the entire group. In addition, if a new technology is employed in a program, it will be demonstrated for Leticia's group. Leticia also suggests that she and her group explore the requirements for technical training awards and set a goal to win such an award in three years.

SENIOR MANAGER

- Missed Opportunity to Address *Information Gathering*

  Max is the CEO of Precision, a midsize manufacturing firm. After graduating college, Max started with the firm in the sales department, then moved on to positions in operations, quality and finance before being named plant manager. He was promoted to CEO two years ago.

  Precision is and has always been inward-focused. It also has always been profitable, although its margins are small. Those small margins have shaped a company culture that is avoidant of discretionary expenses such as external training or professional association memberships. The company's quality control manager once asked Max for the authority to hire an external consultant to address a problem he couldn't solve. Max refused, saying, "Why would I hire a quality expert? That's why I have you." The quality control manager has never asked for outside assistance since.

Now there's a new problem to solve. The company's production team is struggling with an intermittent problem: Its new "fluted" cans are prone to leaks. Each time the fluted cans run on an assembly line, about one percent of them leak after being filled. The company has to dump all the other cans in a pallet when even a single can leaks. The problem appears, then goes away for several days. Frustrated by the waste, the president tells the quality control manager to fix the problem once and for all. Max is starting to field hard questions from his board of directors.

- Developmental Activities to Address *Burke Learning Agility Inventory Self-Assessment* Weakness

Richard leads the board's HR committee, and is also the CEO of a biotech company. He plans to talk to Max about some compensation issues, as well as the quality control problems. In his role as CEO of the biotech company, Richard has learned about learning agility and benchmarking. He tells Max that he wants him to call the biotech company's vendor and arrange to take the *Burke Learning Agility Inventory Self-Assessment*.

Max takes the test, gets his results, and sees that his lowest score is on the dimension of *Information Gathering*. He and the consultant talk about several situations in the past where Max was unsuccessful in resolving a challenge at work, and Max quickly realizes that each involved a lack of *Information Gathering*. He accepts that the test results are accurate.

The consultant, with the support of the Precision board of directors, continues to talk to and work with Max. He asks Max how he might use *Information Gathering* to address the company's quality problem. Max indicates it is time to engage an outside expert. The consultant and Max talk through how Max needs to structure the relationship with the expert as a learning experience for both him and his senior team. Max cannot hire the expert and expect him to fix the problem. The consultant also asks Max to suggest other things he could do to improve in the area of *Information Gathering*. Max and the consultant decide that joining a group of local CEOs from manufacturing companies that meets twice a year would be worth his time. They also agree that for the board to be confident in Max's leadership, he should prepare a presentation for them that outlines the changes he will make to address product quality issues.

CHAPTER 12

FEEDBACK SEEKING

FEEDBACK SEEKING: Asking others for feedback on one's ideas and overall performance

This passage from David McCullough's book, *The Wright Brothers* (2015), takes us to the year 1908. Wilbur Wright is conducting tests in France, and Orville Wright is performing exhibition flights from Fort Myer, an Army base next to Arlington National Cemetery. Orville's plane crashes during one of his flights, and he is badly hurt. He tries to understand the cause of the crash. The "Katharine" mentioned below is the Wrights' sister.

> Meanwhile the Army's Aeronautical Board had begun a formal investigation to determine the cause of the crash. "Orville thinks that the propeller caught in one of the wires connecting the tail to the main part." Katharine wrote. "That also gave a pull on the wings and upset the machine."
>
> As would eventually be determined, Orville was correct. One of the blades on the right propeller had cracked; the propeller began to vibrate; the vibration tore loose a stay wire, which wrapped around the blade, and the broken blade had flown off into the air. Because the stay wire had swerved to brace the rear rudders, they began swerving this way and that and the machine went out of control. (pp. 197-198)

Orville is hospitalized as a result of his injuries. While he is in the hospital, two of his helpers, Charlie Taylor and Charlie Furnas, bring him a piece of the propeller that they had recovered. That broken piece of propeller blade and Orville's conversation with "the two Charlies" give him the feedback he was seeking to adjust his future experiments and performance.

Now we'll look at three scenarios involving individual contributors, managers or senior managers. Each scenario includes an unresolved conflict or problem at work, and has two parts. In the individual contributor scenario, the *Burke Learning Agility Self-Assessment* results are available for you to review, and are used to help the person improve learning agility in the area of *Feedback Seeking*.

The last two scenarios do not include the *Burke Learning Agility Inventory Self-Assessment* bar graph, but do show how to use information from the *Burke Learning Agility Self-Assessment* to create developmental activities that improve **Feedback Seeking** skills.

INDIVIDUAL CONTRIBUTOR

- Missed Opportunity to Address *Feedback Seeking*

Rose is a nurse at a small local hospital that specializes in knee, hip and shoulder replacements. While Rose is very pleasant to her patients, her follow-up response on requests is sporadic. She forgets to bring patients' water to drink and other requested items. In several instances, patients must make requests two times or more before Rose addresses their needs.

Rose and the other nurses on her floor attend an internal seminar on improving patient outcomes. The seminar includes a session where the nurses complete and receive feedback on the *Burke Learning Agility Inventory Self-Assessment*. Rose's profile from her feedback report is shown below. What would be your suggestion to help her use the information from the *Burke Learning Agility Self-Assessment* to improve her performance?

FEEDBACK SEEKING

Rose's Feedback Seeking Score: 15

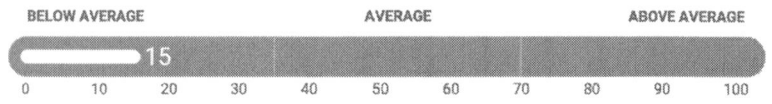

		Norm Group
Behavior 31	Ask peers for feedback on performance	BELOW AVERAGE
Behavior 32	Seek feedback from manager	BELOW AVERAGE
Behavior 33	Discuss potential advancement with manager	BELOW AVERAGE
Behavior 34	Ask others how to improve performance	BELOW AVERAGE

15

- Developmental Activities to Address *Burke Learning Agility Self-Assessment* Weakness

  Rose's lowest score on the assessment is in the area of *Feedback Seeking.* She discusses her assessment results with her supervisor the next day. Her supervisor asks Rose if she thinks the score she received on *Feedback Seeking* is accurate, and Rose replies that it might be, but she's not sure. To find out for sure, Rose's supervisor suggests that she ask each patient in the middle of her shift what she is doing well and what she could be doing better. That way, she can address the items over the rest of her shift. Rose agrees to try this idea out and to discuss the results with her supervisor when they meet next week.

  The next two scenarios are for a manager and a senior manager. In the first part of these examples, the person involved does not have information about learning agility from the *Burke Learning Agility Inventory Self-Assessment.*

In the second part of both examples, the Burke Learning Agility Self-Assessment feedback is known and used to improve a difficult situation at work.

MANAGER

- Missed Opportunity to Address *Feedback Seeking*

Raoul is the head of his hospital's radiology department and manages a team of 10 radiology technicians. Raoul came up through the ranks at the hospital to his current role, which is both managerial and administrative. He has little patient contact. The technicians he supervises are technically proficient, but also are known to text and communicate with friends while they are with patients. Raoul doesn't feel the need to monitor his people's performance since he hasn't received any complaints.

- Developmental Activities to Address *Burke Learning Agility Self-Assessment* Weakness

At this year's professional development seminar, Raoul attends a session on learning agility. As part of the session, he completes the *Burke Learning Agility Self-Assessment* and receives his profile. His lowest dimension on the test is in the area of *Feedback Seeking*.

Raoul meets with his boss after the seminar and brings up his *Burke Learning Agility Self-Assessment* profile. He tells his boss that his *Feedback Seeking* score is probably accurate, because he has never asked his boss, peers or subordinates for their feedback on his work. Raoul assumes they would tell him if there was a problem with his department or his technicians. He's surprised when his boss tells him he was planning to meet with Raoul to discuss turnover in his radiology department, which is 25% higher than in other departments. Raoul agrees that he will ask his people for feedback individually about him as a supervisor and their working conditions, and then summarize what he learns to share with his boss and the group as a whole. He also plans to talk with his peers about how his group might better work with their departments, where appropriate, and to ask how they address turnover. Raoul and his boss decide to discuss next steps in a month.

SENIOR MANAGER

- Missed Opportunity to Address *Feedback Seeking*

Kate is the CEO of a midsize hospital with 300 beds. Kate, like her peers around the country, is faced with diminishing margins, increased regulations as a result of federal health care legislation, and ongoing pressure to acquire or be acquired by other health care entities. Most of her focus is external, although she is hearing from people internally that there are bad relationships among several of her department heads.

- Developmental Activities to Address *Burke Learning Agility Self-Assessment* Weakness

Kate belongs to a professional group of other hospital CEOs who meet twice a year. At the group's spring meeting, she attends a session on the *Burke Learning Agility Self-Assessment* that is facilitated by an external consultant. Participants complete the *Burke Learning Agility Self-Assessment* before their session and receive their feedback at the end. With their feedback in hand, the facilitator suggests participants meet in groups of three to discuss their results.

Kate's lowest score is in the area of *Feedback Seeking*. Following the facilitator's directions, she writes up an example of when her organization was successful in *Feedback Seeking* and one when it was not. The facilitator asks members of each small group to look for connections in their examples that correspond to their *Burke Learning Agility Self-Assessment* results. In her example of a situation that didn't go well, Kate writes about how she failed to smooth out a long-simmering situation that led to a blowup between doctors and nurses. In hindsight, she realizes that

Feedback Seeking might have helped her get to the root cause of the issue before it became a heated conflict. She decides to engage the hospital's vice president of human resources to conduct interviews with a sample of doctors and nurses, and to prepare a summary of the findings. Kate will then participate in a session where results are shared with employees and groups are organized to help solve the problems. She also intends to reinstitute an employee engagement survey to identify issues earlier.

CHAPTER 13

REFLECTING

REFLECTING: Slowing down to evaluate one's own performance to be more effective.

This chapter brings us back to David McCullough's *The Wright Brothers* (2015) for an example of **Reflecting**. The time is 1900, and the Wrights have taken their first trip to Kitty Hawk, NC. They have conducted several tests with their glider. The brothers were struck by the number and variety of birds that filled the air around Kitty Hawk. They observed their flights and took copious notes of what they observed.

> But how did the soaring bird use the wind . . . to sail aloft and bank and turn as it wished? . . .

> The dihedral angle, a shallow v-shape, of the wings was an advantage only in still air, Wilbur wrote. . . .

>> A damp day is unfavorable for soaring unless
>> there is high wind.
>> No bird soars in a calm.

> "All soarers . . . seem to keep their fore-and-aft balance . . . by shifting the center of resistance than by shifting the center of lift," Wilbur wrote.

> For the local citizens, the two brothers from Ohio were extremely hard to figure. . . . "We couldn't help thinking they were just a pair of poor nuts. They'd stand on the beach for hours at a time just looking at the gulls flying, soaring, dipping." Gannets . . . seemed their particular interest.

>> They would watch the gannets and imitate the movements . . . with their arms and hands. They could imitate every movement of the . . . gannets . . . they could move their arms this way and that and bend their elbows and wrist bones up and down . . . just like the gannets. [quote from John T. Daniels]

"Learning the secret of flight from a bird," Orville would say, "was a good deal like learning the secret of magic from a magician." (pp. 52-53)

In this example, the Wright brothers take their time in making observations and to consider how what they are seeing applies to their work as aviators. They reflect on what birds do naturally, and then determine the implications for their efforts.

Our next examples of **Reflecting** are presented in three scenarios, one each involving an individual contributor, manager or senior manager. Each scenario has two parts and involves a conflict or issue the person is experiencing at work. The individual contributor example includes a graph showing the *Burke Learning Agility Inventory Self-Assessment* results for the person. The last two scenarios do not include the bar graph, but show how using information from the *Burke Learning Agility Self-Assessment* can help improve the person's weakness in **Reflecting**.

INDIVIDUAL CONTRIBUTOR

- Missed Opportunity to Address *Reflecting*

    Greg works 12-hour shifts as a production-line operator in a factory that produces widgets. A production report is created on the line's performance after each shift with information on metrics such as output and rejects. Each day's reports are combined for the week and the month, and shared with operators in their weekly production meetings. The operators and their supervisors don't do anything with the information in the reports, and Greg is never asked by his supervisor to reflect on how he might improve his job performance.

    Greg's crew works a swing shift, which means that every two weeks they switch from day shift to night shift. During the transition from days to nights, there is a four-hour period for training. At the most recent training session, Greg completes and receives feedback on the *Burke Learning Agility Inventory Self-Assessment*. Greg's *Burke Learning Agility Self-Assessment* feedback report profile is shown below. How would you suggest that Greg use the information from the *Burke Learning Agility Self-Assessment* to improve his performance on the production line?

REFLECTING

Greg's Reflecting Score: 10

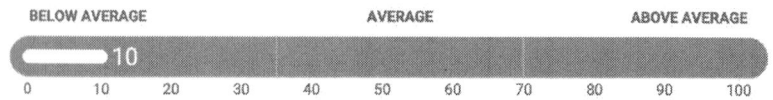

			Norm Group
Behavior 35	Reflect on work processes and projects		BELOW AVERAGE
Behavior 36	Reflect on how to be more effective		BELOW AVERAGE
Behavior 37	Consider reasons for and consequences of actions and events		BELOW AVERAGE
Behavior 38	Evaluate events with others to understand what happened		BELOW AVERAGE

- Developmental Activities to Address *Burke Learning Agility Self-Assessment* Weakness

Greg meets with his supervisor right after training ends and shares his *Burke Learning Agility Inventory Self-Assessment* report. Greg tells his supervisor that he agrees that *Reflecting* is not one of his strengths, as his *Burke Learning Agility Self-Assessment* results show. Greg's supervisor asks if Greg has any ideas about what he could do to increase his score in the area of *Reflecting*. Greg mentions the reports that the crew on his line receives each week regarding their performance, and suggests that he could keep notes of things he observes during his shifts. He offers to bring his notes along with the production results for the last two weeks to an upcoming weekly meeting. He suggests that he and his peers could focus individually on how they could use the information to improve the production on their lines. His supervisor says he will follow Greg's suggestion so that everyone on the shift can work to improve their production results.

Next we have scenarios for a manager and a senior manager who are facing unresolved difficulties at work. In the first part of each example, information from the *Burke Learning Agility Inventory Self-Assessment* is not available. In the second part, the *Burke Learning Agility Self-Assessment* feedback is known and used to improve each situation.

MANAGER

- Missed Opportunity to Address *Reflecting*

    Alicia is a project manager at a consulting firm that is working on a change-management project for a public-sector agency. The project involves business process re-engineering. The beginning of the project requires a heavy amount of analytic work, including planning of responsibilities, deliverables and due dates. The output of this effort is a project plan that is constantly used for decision-making and frequently updated. The process used to make these changes at the top of the organization is to be repeated as the process cascades downward. A lot of effort is put into planning, but the project leaders never seem to find time to reflect on what did and didn't work at each level in the organization.

- Developmental Activities to Address *Burke Learning Agility Self-Assessment* Weakness

In order to maintain her project management certification, Alicia must attend eight hours of training each year. One of this year's training sessions is devoted to learning agility, and Alicia has an opportunity to complete the *Burke Learning Agility Inventory Self-Assessment* and receive feedback. Alicia's lowest learning agility dimension on the *Burke Learning Agility Self-Assessment* is *Reflecting*. As she thinks about it, which she doesn't normally do, she agrees that her score is accurate. She discusses the results with the facilitator, and mentions that her weakest dimension also seems to be a weakness for her firm as a whole. The facilitator is not surprised, as he indicates that the environment someone works in can affect their learning agility profile.

Alicia tells the facilitator about the project she is leading, and he asks if there is a way to build *Reflecting* into the project. She says she probably could establish an opportunity for *Reflecting* at the end of the implementation at each level. Alicia and the facilitator talk more about how that would work. Alicia is excited about figuring it out, and spends the rest of the session working on a presentation to the firm's senior management on how the organization can incorporate *Reflecting* at each stage of her project and the benefits that may be realized.

SENIOR MANAGER

- Missed Opportunity to Address *Reflecting*

Yolanda is the vice president of strategy and acquisition integration for a Fortune 500 consumer products company. Her group is charged with finding acquisition targets and determining which have the most synergy and upside potential. Her group then presents its recommendations to senior management for approval. With senior management's agreement, Yolanda's group then closes the deal and leads the integration of the new company into the mother company.

This has been a busy year for Yolanda and her team, and there has been no time for *Reflecting* on what went well on each closed deal or what could be improved for the next acquisition. Instead, there is too much focus on the next acquisition in the pipeline and on completing the due diligence process. The unrelenting pace proves unsustainable when an acquisition that seemed to be a sure thing falls apart at the very end of the process—even as Yolanda's group is beginning to plan how to integrate the new company. Yolanda's team was moving so quickly that it was already planning integration around the new company. The CEO tells Yolanda that she is not willing to get that far on a deal and lose out again.

- Developmental Activities to Address *Burke Learning Agility Self-Assessment* Weakness

Yolanda, like the company's CEO, is very disappointed about the deal's unravelling. She reaches out to her mentor from business school, and he connects her with Peter, a faculty member who is doing research on learning agility.

Peter arranges for Yolanda to complete and receive feedback on the *Burke Learning Agility Inventory Self-Assessment*. Yolanda learns that her highest score is in the area of *Speed*, and her lowest score is in the area of *Reflecting*. Yolanda is willing to explore whether this is accurate, and discusses a few previous work projects with the professor. A review of the failed acquisition gives Yolanda all the information she needs, and she agrees that her *Reflecting* score is accurate. She and Peter talk about how *Reflecting* could be used to review why the acquisition attempt was not successful. Yolanda and Peter also discuss how she could take this approach back to her CEO and get his support to implement a process for *Reflecting* on the most recent failure and on all successful or unsuccessful acquisitions going forward.

SECTION III

INTEGRATION OF THE *BURKE LEARNING AGILITY SELF-ASSESSMENT* INTO VARIOUS HR DISCIPLINES

When the *Burke Learning Agility Inventory* was introduced in February 2016, there was a lot of excitement, particularly from students of Dr. Warner Burke who had watched the evolution of the *Burke Learning Agility Self-Assessment* from an idea to an actual product. Before long, Burke and the product's developers at EASI•Consult began to get questions from potential users who wanted to know how and when to use the *Burke Learning Agility Inventory Self-Assessment*. It became obvious that organizations wanted to learn about specific ways that the *Burke Learning Agility Self-Assessment* can be used with employees and employee groups. That is the purpose of Section 3 of this book. The chapters that follow will outline ideas for incorporating the *Burke Learning Agility Inventory Self-Assessment* into training or orientation programs, individual assessments, performance management and development, succession planning, coaching and organizational development interventions.

CHAPTER 14

INTEGRATING THE *BURKE LEARNING AGILITY SELF-ASSESSMENT REPORT* INTO TRAINING, ORIENTATION AND INDUCTION PROGRAMS

USING THE *BURKE LEARNING AGILITY SELF-ASSESSMENT REPORT* FOR TRAINING, ORIENTATION AND INDUCTION PROGRAMS

Orientation, if done in a group format, is a specific type of training program. Both orientation and induction were mentioned in the title of this chapter because induction into an organization can be the opportunity to connect what happens in selection to the rest of a person's experience as an employee. Too often, selection and induction, or training, are separate and distinct processes. There is typically little to no attempt to apply what is learned in the selection process to an employee's induction, "onboarding" or orientation.

This is a lost opportunity. For example, if a job candidate was your first choice among available applicants, and scored a satisfactory but not outstanding score in the screening capability of working well with others, why would you not want to share that development need with the candidate during induction? You and the new employee could talk about what working well with others looks like in your organization and discuss ways that your new employee could build his or her skills in this area during the induction period and beyond.

The *Burke Learning Agility Inventory Self-Assessment* could also be used as a pre-work assignment for people attending an induction or another training program. What if one of your new employees took the *Burke Learning Agility Self-Assessment* and found that one of his or her weakest areas was **Interpersonal Risk Taking**? This tells you that your new employee is not comfortable taking risks when it involves relating to other people. Your new hire may be shy or introverted. He or she is not inclined to reach out, particularly in a new situation. In fact, reaching out may be uncomfortable for your new hire *in any situation.*

Let's assume that you combine the information gathered during the selection process with the assessment data from the *Burke Learning Agility Self-Assessment*, which was given as part of the pre-work process for orientation. In the interview, you may have learned that your new employee needs to strengthen his or her ability to work as part of a team. In the orientation pre-work, you may learn about a learning agility weakness in **Interpersonal Risk Taking**. How can you use that information during orientation to make this employee more effective in the future? How can you encourage that employee to take interpersonal risks to build more effective relationships with other members of his or her team?

COMPETENCY ACQUISITION PROCESS

One of the frameworks we used at EASI•Consult, now Burke Assessments, to help people improve a skill in a specific area is called the Competency Acquisition Process (Boyatzis, 1982). This framework grew out of the work of McBer & Company (now Korn Ferry Hay Group) and has stood the test of time. There are five steps in the process: 1) Recognition; 2) Understanding; 3) Self-Assessment; 4) Skill Practice; 5) Practice on the Job.

Let's revisit our induction example on the previous page to show this process in action. If the learning agility skill we are working on is *Interpersonal Risk Taking*, in the first step of the Recognition stage, you want your employee to be able to identify an example from a case study or description of someone demonstrating *Interpersonal Risk Taking*.

In Step 2, Understanding, you clearly define the different aspects of *Interpersonal Risk Taking*. The employee should now know what *Interpersonal Risk Taking* is as we have defined it.

Step 3 involves assessing yourself against the standard of *Interpersonal Risk Taking*. In this situation, an organization would administer the *Burke Learning Agility Self-Assessment* to measure an employee's *Interpersonal Risk Taking* skills.

In Step 4, the person practices *Interpersonal Risk Taking* and receives feedback. Practice opportunities can be created in the induction or training program for the person to allow him or her to try new behaviors in a safe environment. Typically, there is a discussion after the practice session about what the person did well and the things he or she can do to continue to improve.

Step 5 involves practice on the job. The things that the person learned in step four are what he or she brings along to include in their improvement plans at the end of the induction or training program. For example, what specific opportunity will the person have in the near future to continue to work on developing that skill? Ideally, the person's supervisor is included in this discussion. The supervisor can help create situations where the employee can continue to get better at *Interpersonal Risk Taking*. This also can become part of the employee's development plan, which can be found in Chapter 16 on Performance Management.

The Competency Acquisition Process is a useful five-step approach that allows you to make sure you are addressing all aspects necessary to help a person improve his or her skills in a particular area. Now let's take a step back, and up, to view how the *Burke Learning Agility Inventory Self-Assessment* can be used strategically as part of an induction or other training program.

USING THE *BURKE LEARNING AGILITY SELF-ASSESSMENT REPORT* AS A DIAGNOSTIC TOOL FOR TRAINING

When the *Burke Learning Agility Self-Assessment* is used as part of the pre-work process for a training program, the trainers should receive the test results before the session. This will allow them to better know their audience individually and as a group. *Burke Learning Agility Self-Assessment* content is best positioned in the training after any introductory or overview material about the training course is presented.

The trainer should provide a brief explanation of learning agility theory and how the *Burke Learning Agility Self-Assessment* was developed. The trainers could show participants an example of a *Burke Learning Agility Inventory Self-Assessment* Feedback Report. He or she might ask participants to predict what their two highest and two lowest dimensions will be when they receive their own feedback.

The trainer should then give participants their feedback reports. After giving participants a few minutes to review the information, the facilitators should circulate and talk to participants individually about their reactions to their feedback reports. Questions could include: "Does this report describe you?" or "Did anything surprise you?" The trainer should then make some summary comments, share group-level data when applicable, and offer participants an opportunity to ask questions.

In a group setting, here are a few examples of questions to ask:

- If someone scored low on one of the dimensions, what would that look like on the job?
- If someone scored high on one dimension and low on a seemingly similar one, how could that be? For example, scoring low on

Interpersonal Risk Taking and scoring high on *Collaborating* may seem contradictory at first glance. The trainer should encourage members of the group to come up with a hypothetical example of what that would look like if it were happening on the job.

- Using a composite profile for the group, ask, "What will be difficult for us, as trainers, to get you to do?" For example, if based on the composite the group was low on *Interpersonal Risk Taking*, they might resist working in small groups where they have to critique each other's work. Another question might be, "What aspects of the training will be easy for you based on the group composite?"

Let's take that last question and expand on what might happen during the training session. If *Reflecting* was low for the group, it might be difficult to get participants to reflect on what they learned during the previous day. The trainer should think about what activities are required in the training session, such as small group work or simulations. The trainer should make a connection between activities in the class or other dimensions and where there might be a chance to practice a learning agility dimension. The training environment is a safe place in which to practice. A role-playing exercise could be an opportunity to work on *Performance Risk Taking*. A similar exercise with small groups of two or three people could be an opportunity to work on *Interpersonal Risk Taking* or other dimensions.

At the end of the training session, the trainer should encourage participants to consider the areas of learning agility that they need to strengthen as they set their performance goals and development plans. Participants also should think about incorporating their learning agility strengths in those plans.

In the next chapter, we will examine how to use the *Burke Learning Agility Inventory Self-Assessment* as part of an individual assessment process.

CHAPTER 15

INTEGRATING THE *BURKE LEARNING AGILITY SELF-ASSESSMENT REPORT* INTO INDIVIDUAL ASSESSMENTS

Assessments are how organizations obtain information about a person to make a more informed decision about who to hire and what to develop, typically in terms of leadership skills or competencies. The two basic types of assessments are assessments for selection and assessments for development. In this chapter, we will look at the two types of assessments and discuss how each is unique. We also will discuss the typical components found in each type of assessment, and examine how the *Burke Learning Agility Self-Assessment* can add to each type of assessment.

In any assessment, we are trying to find the best match or "fit" between a person, their skills, abilities and competencies and the requirements of a job.

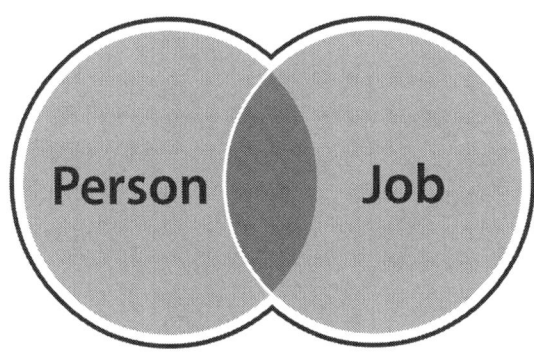

When you are looking at the job side of the equation, you have several ways to ensure that the job-person match is a good one. For example, you can:

- Use a job description to determine the position's duties and responsibilities.
- Ask the supervisor of the person who is being hired if there are any challenges or changes in the job that are not listed in the description.
- Ask the previous job holder about what skills and duties were required in the job.
- Talk to people who know about the job or have worked with a person who held the job about the tasks and skills required to do it well.

In our work as consultants, we collect that information through something called a **Job Analysis Questionnaire (JAQ)**. This allows our firm, EASI•Consult, now Burke Assessments, to establish "best fit ranges" across several dimensions that are determined to be important for the job. It is during this process of collecting information about the job from subject matter experts that we also learn if there are specific competencies that are important for the job. We also typically find out through this process if there are certain learning agility dimensions, like *Flexibility* or *Collaborating*, that may be important for success. At a point, we aggregate the information we have about the job and create a profile of "best fit" against which to compare and assess candidates.

The circle below describes the components that need to be assembled and considered on the job side of the assessment equation.

ASSESSMENT FOR SELECTION

If an assessment is being done for selection purposes, we are most likely assessing several candidates to determine which one is the best fit for the position. The ultimate decision will be made by the hiring manager, but this process brings data to that discussion.

There can be several variables that might impact what components are included in an assessment battery. The two biggest variables are time and cost. A typical assessment battery for Burke Assessments would include:

- Cognitive Ability – Watson-Glaser™, for example
- Personality Inventory – Hogan / Jackson, for example
- Learning Agility – *Burke Learning Agility Inventory Self-Assessment*
- Structured Behavioral Interview – A formalized interview in which candidates are asked a consistent set of competency-based questions to get specific examples from the individual's experience of where they demonstrated a competency. An example of this might be, "Tell me about a time when you did xyz on the job. What exactly did you say and do and what was the outcome?"
- Simulations or Case Study – This is an optional assessment component in which candidates are given information about a fictitious company that is facing real-world issues or challenges. The candidates must role-play as employees and discuss how they would address the issues. Typically, a consultant role-plays the part of a senior manager within the fictitious organization.

ILLUSTRATION 1: ASSESSMENT FOR SELECTION PROCESS DIAGRAM

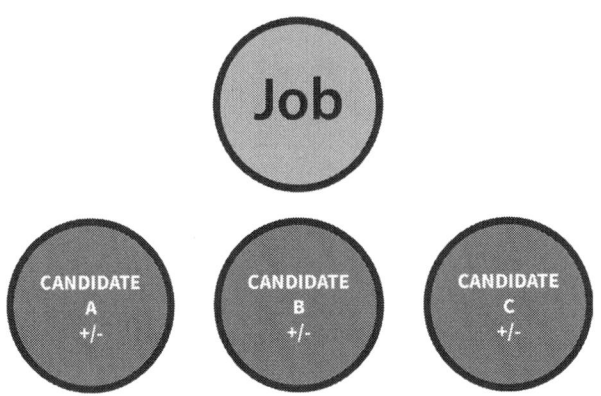

If the assessment is for selection, Burke Assessments prepares a separate assessment report for each candidate. It includes a brief, high-level overview of the candidate's fit with as much or as little additional detail as the company requests. Additionally, the level and detail of data provided depends on an individual client's preferences and needs.

After submitting the applicant report, Burke Assessments' assessors meet in person or by phone with an organization's hiring manager and a human resources representative, if requested. Burke Assessments' role is not to advocate for a specific candidate, but to use data to describe each individual candidate's strengths as well as issues his or her supervisor would likely need to manage. The Burke Assessments assessor would discuss each candidate with the hiring manager until he or she is clear about each candidates' strengths and shortcomings relative to the job *(see Illustration 2)*. At this point, the strengths and potential gaps based on relevant competencies will have been thoroughly described. Here is an illustration of how the process works:

CANDIDATE EVALUATION DISCUSSION

A hiring manager is faced with selecting one of three candidates. Each brings a combination of strengths and weaknesses. How would you review the information to reach a decision?

According to the data from Burke Assessments' assessor, the overriding issue in the hiring decision hinges on *Flexibility*. Candidates A and B both scored on the high end of Rigidity on the Personality Test and low on *Flexibility* on the *Burke Learning Agility Self-Assessment*. In their structured interviews, the previous work situations they described involved success in modifying their opinion about something. The hiring manager felt those were weak examples. Candidate C, the third candidate, didn't demonstrate *Collaborating*. In his interview, he discussed an opportunity he had to collaborate on a project and his decision to instead work alone. His learning agility score on *Collaborating* was in the high/medium range. The hiring manager thought all three were strong candidates, but that he could more easily address the *Collaborating* issue with Candidate C than the *Flexibility* issue with candidates A and B. After Candidate C was hired, he met with the Burke Assessments' assessor to review his assessment results. The hiring manager then followed up and put his new employee on a project requiring *Collaborating*. The two of them met weekly to discuss the project (see *Illustration 2* below).

ILLUSTRATION 2: CANDIDATE COMPARISON

Candidate A
- High Rigidity on Hogan Assessment
- Low *Flexibility* on *Burke Learning Agility Self-Assessments*
- SI weak example of modifying opinion

Candidate B
- High Rigidity on Hogan Assessment
- Low *Flexibility* on *Burke Learning Agility Self-Assessments*
- SI weak example of modifying opinion

Candidate C
- No concerns on Hogan Assessment
- Med/Hi *Collaborating* on Burke Learning Agility Self-Assessments
- Didn't demonstrate *Collaborating* on Structured Interviews

Company selected Candidate C. Determined it would be easier to further develop *Collaborating* in Candidate C than to try to modify the Rigidity/*Flexibility* in Candidates A and B.

ASSESSMENT FOR DEVELOPMENT

Assessments for development involve assessing an existing employee. The development need may be for the person to be more effective in his or her current job, or it may be in preparation for a future position. Often, assessment for development is used to identify or develop leadership potential and skills. If the developmental assessment is for a future or higher-level position, the person being assessed may not know what that position is. We will talk about this in the context of succession planning in Chapter 17. In the case of a developmental assessment, the person may only be told, "You are a person with potential. If you have interest in being considered for additional responsibility in the future, we would like you to go through this process."

If the position is known, then the process for collecting information about the job side of the equation is the same as is used for selection assessment earlier in this chapter. Many of the tools would be the same for the person side of the assessment:

- **Cognitive Ability – Watson-Glaser™ Critical Thinking Appraisal, for example**
- **Personality Inventory – Hogan, for example**
- **Learning Agility –** *Burke Learning Agility Inventory Self-Assessment*
- **Competencies**
  - **Structured Interview**
  - **360-Degree Leadership Feedback Survey**
- **Demonstration of skills and abilities – simulation or case study**

The results of assessments for development are summarized into a detailed report. Particularly in the case of assessment for selection, an executive summary may be prepared for the candidate selected, while his or her boss may receive a more detailed version. In assessment for development, the assessor typically sends the report to the employee and schedules a meeting to discuss the results within a few days. The purpose of the meeting is for the employee to ask questions and understand what the report means, but not justify or defend any information in it. The employee's HR manager often sits in on the initial feedback meeting to ask clarifying questions the organization might have about the report.

Many organizations request a second meeting with the assessor, the supervisor and the employee who was assessed. Typically, the person who was assessed leads that session by telling the boss what he or she learned. The assessor is available to clarify or provide commentary on the content of the report. The intent of the meeting is to provide an opportunity for the supervisor and the employee who is being assessed to identify an assignment that will allow the employee to work on his or her development needs. To be effective, the discussion should include what competencies, learning agility dimensions or leadership styles the employee should demonstrate in the future. The discussion should also include setting goals and timelines. In some instances, the organization may ask the employee to apply what he or she learned during the assessment process to an individual development plan, and to share ideas with his or her supervisor during the meeting.

The conversation is a little different if the assessment for development is intended to prepare an employee to move to the next level in an organization. The goal of that assessment process is to gauge whether the employee is able to demonstrate certain competencies, learning agility dimensions or leadership styles through specific assignments or projects. The employee who is being assessed should understand that completing a project or activity would demonstrate the capabilities of someone at the next level. If the person was successful in showing those capabilities, he or she would be deemed ready for additional responsibilities.

In either the case of development for a current position or for a future position, an individual has the opportunity to develop learning agility dimensions not already in his or her repertoire. But it is important for the person to be aware that performance on this project may suffer as he or she attempts to use a learning agility dimension that is uncomfortable and in which the person is not proficient.

CHAPTER 16

INTEGRATING THE *BURKE LEARNING AGILITY INVENTORY SELF-ASSESSMENT REPORT* INTO PERFORMANCE MANAGEMENT AND DEVELOPMENT

PERFORMANCE MANAGEMENT AND DEVELOPMENT

The two HR disciplines of performance management and development are being presented in this chapter as one continuous process, although a case could be made that these are two independent aspects of HR. Both positions are correct. Organizations that are more talent-management focused will integrate performance management and development and treat it as one seamless process. These same organizations will have a separate function focused on training, leadership and other applications of development.

In many organizations, performance management is "owned" by the compensation function. When performance management and development are presented as a single process, the talent management team will work with compensation so that the company's beliefs about development are presented consistently throughout.

In the performance management section of this chapter, we're going to describe what might happen as we review the fictitious character of Eliza and her performance over the last 12 months. The discussion of her performance will lead us to set objectives for the next 12 months. When we move to the development portion of the chapter, we will use both the objectives (the "what") and competencies (the "how") from last year's performance, together with next year's objectives, to set Eliza's development plan for the coming year.

Let's assume that the *Burke Learning Agility Self-Assessment* was not a factor in creating the past year's development plan. But Eliza has taken the *Burke Learning Agility Self-Assessment* recently, and is asked to bring her report to her performance review meeting.

PERFORMANCE MANAGEMENT

Like many companies, the organization Eliza works for uses a rating scale of Exceeds, Meets or Below Expectations to rate an employee's overall performance. At Burke Assessments, our experience is that 85% of employees at any organization will meet expectations. We define this broadly as an employee doing what he or she has been asked (objectives) and doing it (how) in the way which he or she was asked. About 10% of an organization's employees will exceed expectations, which we define as accomplishing their objectives and doing so in a way that far exceeds everyone else. The other five percent of employees will be below expectations in the "how" or "what," and that is how they will be rated. Those employees will be informed that their performance must improve or they will lose their jobs.

At Eliza's performance review meeting, objectives for her will be discussed and evaluated using the three-point scale. We will acknowledge when her performance has been good. We'll also mention or solicit from her things that did not go well or could be improved. We'll carry this information forward into the next year's objectives and development plan for Eliza.

As a consulting firm, our bias is to weigh how objectives are accomplished equally with what was accomplished. Burke Assessments uses competencies to define the "what" and assigns three to five behavioral descriptions to each competency. As we review Eliza's performance this year, we'll look at the "how" and talk to her about the behaviors that she demonstrated, as well as those that could be improved or were not demonstrated. We'll capture all this information and include it in her development plan for next year.

After that, we'll review Eliza's development plan from the year just completed and discuss it with her. If there are any elements in the plan that were not completed and still need to be done, we'll note them and include them in the development discussion for the coming year.

What follows is an example of Eliza's performance appraisal form for this past year. This is what we'll review with her.

PERFORMANCE APPRAISAL FORM
(Past 12 Months)

Name: *Eliza Employee*   **Reviewer's Name:** *Joe Boss*
Position: *Inside Sales Support*   **Date**: *Today*

Objective 1: *Eliza is involved with supporting the sales of $5 million of product to customers A, B and C.*

Exceeds: ☐   Meets: ☒   Below ☐

Competencies:

Relationship Building

☒ Develops relationships to accomplish work

☒ Maintains self-control under pressure

☐ Maintains objectivity when there is not agreement between self and others

Exceeds: ☐   Meets: ☒   Below ☐

Next is the Performance Appraisal Form for the following 12 months.

PERFORMANCE APPRAISAL FORM
(Future 12 Months)

Name: *Eliza Employee*   **Reviewer's Name:** *Joe Boss*
Position: *Inside Sales Support*   **Date:** *Today*

Objective 1: *Eliza is involved with supporting the sales of $5 million of product to customers A, B and C.*

     Exceeds: ☐   Meets: ☐   Below ☐

Objective 2: *Eliza will develop a relationship with customer D, Don Spiegal, that will result in new sales of $500,000.*

*Note: Relationship building and the other competencies will be rated at the time of the next performance review in 12 months. The development plan part of the appraisal (usually on the back page of the two-page form) will be covered in the second part of this chapter on development. Eliza's development plan will include attending a negotiations skills class, applying what she learned to develop a relationship with customer D, Don Spiegal, that will translate into sales of $500,000. Eliza's learning agility opportunities of **Collaborating** and **Interpersonal Risk Taking** also will be addressed.*

DEVELOPMENT

The first part of the performance or development conversation involves performance over the last 12 months. We just finished that part of the conversation. We need to look forward to what objectives Eliza should accomplish next year and how she will develop the skills, behaviors or competencies necessary to reach those goals. You'll see references to the "what" and the "how" later in this chapter.

> ## ITEMS TO BRING TO THE DEVELOPMENT PLANNING DISCUSSION
>
> There are some tools/pieces of information that can support our development conversation.
>
> 1. Performance appraisal form for the past year.
> 2. New performance appraisal form for the new fiscal year.
> 3. Competency/development in place document (a separate document from the appraisal form).
> 4. Eliza's *Burke Learning Agility Self-Assessment* Profile and any other assessment or training data the employee acquired over the past year.

Now that we have everything together, let's look at how we'll use these tools to create Eliza's development plan for the coming 12 months.

1. Last year's performance appraisal form (see p165). We know Eliza has "met" our expectations. Her performance is adequate. She has accomplished the objectives set for her in the previous year.

   In Eliza's situation, we are only looking at the competency of Building Relationships. A typical competency model might have eight to 10 competencies. As her supervisor, we might assess all the competencies for Eliza, but only focus on the three to five competencies where she has room for improvement. In Eliza's case, we determined that the part of Building Relationships where there was room for improvement was in *Maintains objectivity when there is not agreement between self and others* (see p165). This is something we want to bring forward and include in the planning of objectives and her development plan for the coming year.

2. Performance appraisal form for the new fiscal year (see p166). We saw Eliza's performance as "meets expectations" for last year. We want to ask her to perform at a higher level in the coming year. We may assign a few more customers to her and set specific objectives around serving them well. We may also ask that she improve her service to existing customers as another performance objective. Once the objectives have been set, we need to focus on the "how," of the development plan, that comes next. In Eliza's case, there is room for improvement in

Maintains objectivity when there is not agreement between self and others. We receive Eliza's information from the competency/development in place document, which is described below.

3. Competency/development in place document. (see below). This document has indexed every behavioral description for the company's competency model; only a small piece of the document is shown here. We need to identify more information on a specific assignment that will help Eliza strengthen the behavior of Maintaining objectivity where there is not agreement between self and others. The list of options appears in the lower part of the box below.

The index below shows development in place assignments 4, 7, 11, 28 and 55 in the developmental activities section. These suggestions are not intended to be prescriptive, but to start the discussion with Eliza. We decide to spend time discussing how we might use #4 – *Handle a negotiation with a customer* and #55 – *Make peace with an enemy* (see below).

COMPETENCY DEVELOPMENT IN PLACE DOCUMENT

Building Relationships

Develops relationships to accomplish work.	1, 7, 26-28
Maintains self-control under pressure.	34, 48, 55
Maintains objectivity when there is not agreement between self and others.	4, 7, 11, 28, 55

Developmental In-Place Assignments

1 – Task force on a pressing business problem
4 – Handle a negotiation with a customer
7 – Integrate systems across units
11 – Go off-site to troubleshoot problems (deal with dissatisfied customers)
26 – Serve on new project / product review committee
27 – Work short periods in other units
28 – Do a project with another function
34 – Assign project with tight deadline
48 – Deal with a business crisis
55 – Make peace with an enemy

Development assignment #4, *Handle a negotiation with a customer.* With development assignment 4, Eliza agrees that she will attend a negotiation skills class in the first quarter. She will then handle the negotiations for a contract with her new customer, Don Spiegal. Spiegal is also performance objective 2, the new customer we gave her (see p166).

Development assignment #55, *Make peace with an enemy.* This is an example of identifying an "unofficial" part of a development plan. Eliza struggles to address difficulties with people she doesn't respect. She is willing to work on this area, but would like to do it in a way that doesn't count against her performance this year. This is a judgement call, but provides an illustration of a learning goal. It could also be structured as a performance goal. Eliza agrees that if she makes progress in this area this year, she will include this in her development plan as a performance goal for the following year. At that point, she will be assessed on her performance in this area for one of her customers.

This idea of a learning goal versus a performance goal is one that Carol Dweck (2006) describes in her book *Mindset.* She contends that people have either fixed or growth mindsets. People with fixed mindsets believe their qualities are carved in stone, while people with growth mindsets believe that their basic qualities are things they can cultivate through their efforts. In her book, Dweck writes about studies that show that people with fixed mindsets are terrible at understanding their ability and their performance. According to Dweck, "The fixed mindset makes you concerned with how you'll be judged, the growth mindset makes you concerned with improving." (p. 13)

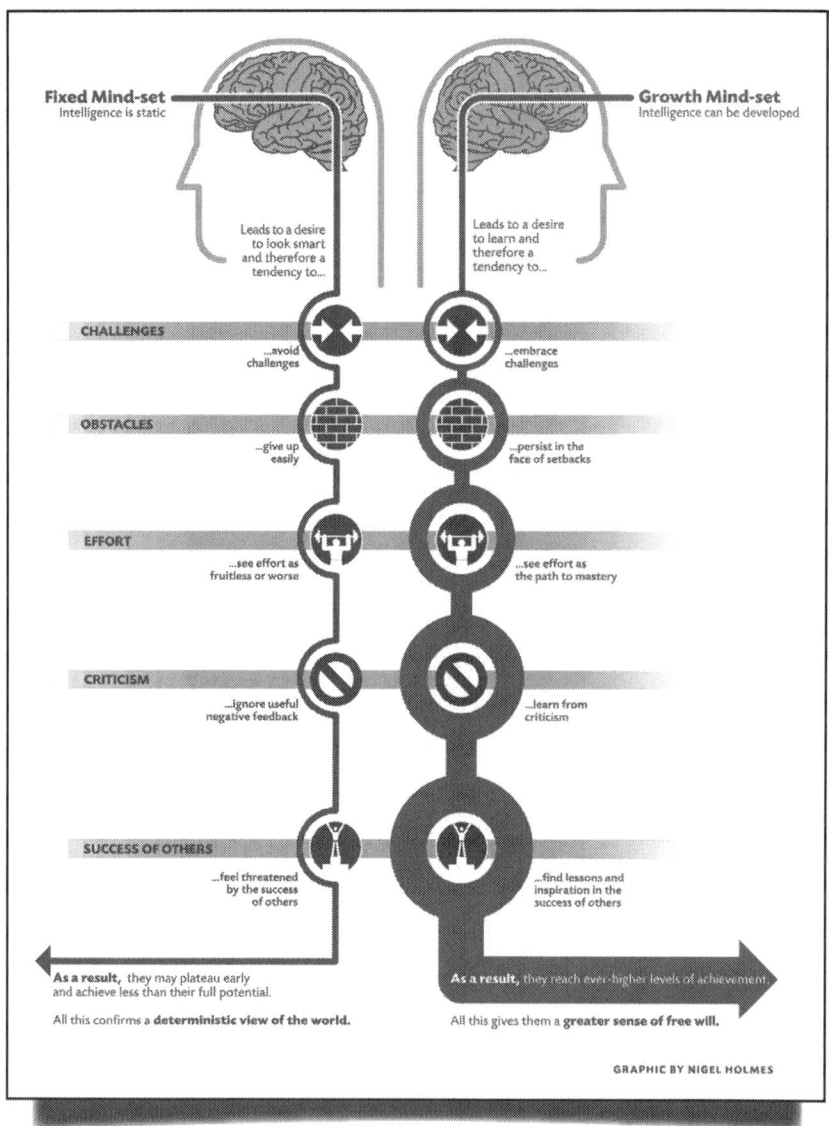

From Mindset by C. Dweck, 2006, New York: Ballantine Books. Copyright 2006 by Carol S. Dweck, Ph.D. Reprinted with permission.

We are now going to return to Eliza and continue looking at her development plan as we address learning agility.

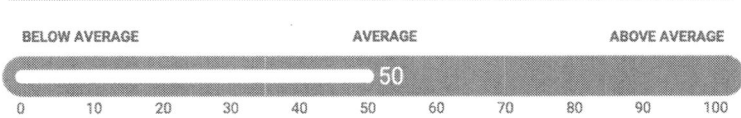

Your Learning Agility Scores

Eliza Dowell – 2024-06-25 (GMT)

BELOW AVERAGE	AVERAGE	ABOVE AVERAGE

50

0 10 20 30 40 50 60 70 80 90 100

Overall Score Interpretation

Your score, at the 50th percentile, reflects a solid average score as compared to the norm (comparison) group indicated above. Compared with peers from this group, you display a good level of flexibility, skills, and motivation. Your capacity to apply agile behavior in learning situations is consistent, and with just a bit more focus, you can further enhance your agility and adaptability.

Subscale Scores

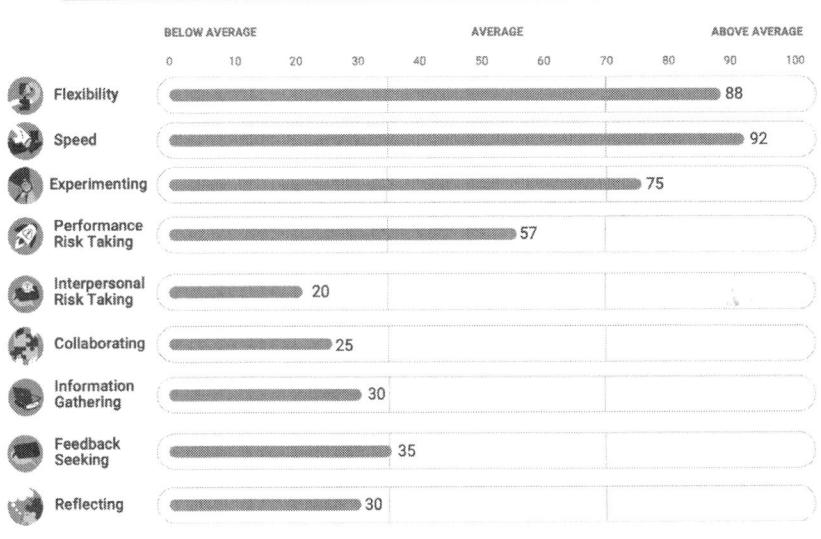

	BELOW AVERAGE			AVERAGE				ABOVE AVERAGE	
	0 10	20	30	40 50	60	70	80	90	100
Flexibility								88	
Speed								92	
Experimenting							75		
Performance Risk Taking					57				
Interpersonal Risk Taking		20							
Collaborating		25							
Information Gathering			30						
Feedback Seeking			35						
Reflecting			30						

The last consideration for Eliza's development plan is learning agility. We've included Eliza's profile from her *Burke Learning Agility Self-Assessment* report, which shows that her two lowest dimensions are **Collaborating** and Interpersonal Risk Taking. This information appears to be consistent with the competency Eliza needs to improve, **Building Relationships**, and the learning agility dimensions which she finds most challenging, **Interpersonal Risk Taking** and **Collaborating**.

The definition of **Collaborating** from the *Burke Learning Agility Self-Assessment* is "finding ways to work with others that generates unique opportunities for learning." Eliza is going to work with others as she works on her customer relationships. **Interpersonal Risk Taking** from the *Burke Learning Agility Self-Assessment* is defined as "discussing differences with others in ways that result in learning and change." Eliza decides that she is going to do this by making peace with an enemy in her personal life, not in her professional life. There is someone in her neighborhood who she won't talk to because of a difference of opinion, but now they must work together on a community project.

In the next year, we will talk regularly with Eliza about what she learns in dealings with her neighbor, with the agreement that it will not be factored into her formal performance evaluation. Dweck would identify this as a learning goal for Eliza. The following year, working on a difficult relationship with a customer will be part of her formal evaluation.

The intent of this chapter was to give you a better idea of how to integrate learning agility into performance management and development. Development should never mean just sending someone to training classes. Although training can be part of a larger development experience, it also must be applied on the job. For most employees at most companies, development occurs on the job, using job experiences. The job experiences can and should be connected to competencies, and knowing which competencies will support a job experience will provide greater clarity to each aspect of the developmental process.

Learning agility can give people insight into how flexible they are as learners. It also helps them understand what aspects of learning agility come easily for them, and what aspects are more challenging. Working on development activities and using learning agility to develop skills that feel uncomfortable hold the most promise for increasing an individual's learning agility. In the next chapter, we will look at learning agility as part of decision-making in succession planning.

CHAPTER 17

INTEGRATING THE *BURKE LEARNING AGILITY SELF-ASSESSMENT REPORT* INTO SUCCESSION PLANNING

This chapter will help explain how the *Burke Learning Agility Inventory Self-Assessment* can be used to support succession planning. To accomplish this, we need to describe some fundamental aspects of typical succession planning efforts.

Successful succession planning involves individual assessments; as a reminder, there is extensive information on individual assessments and assessment reports in Chapter 15 of this book.

Any discussion of succession planning should start by defining terms and language used in the process. At Burke Assessments, when we work on succession planning, we think in terms of talent pools. This differs from the old way of doing succession planning, which used what was then called "replacement charting." Organizations that used replacement charting for succession planning typically kept a thick book of charts that showed the senior roles in the organization, the names of the person in each role, the names of each person's replacement, and those successors' development plans. This book of charts and names was reviewed by the organization's senior managers once a year. Otherwise, it was rarely referred to, even when a position opened in the company and a replacement was needed to fill that role. Because the charts were rarely used as intended, this approach to succession planning eventually fell out of favor.

Next came a shift in thinking and the development of talent pools, in which all employees have a development plan that is an output of the performance appraisal process. The talent pool typically covers critical jobs in an organization, such as plant manager, account manager or chief financial officer. People who are candidates for these critical roles receive more attention and more in-depth development plans. Each critical position has a "pool" of candidates who are being developed to move into one or more key roles. These pools are typically two to three times the flow rate, which means if an organization typically replaces two plant managers a year, it should have four to six people in the plant manager talent pool.

With the talent pool model, organizations can decide whether or not to tell current employees that they are in a pool for a particular job. At a minimum, employees should be told that the organization has tapped them as having potential. Further, potential should be defined for employees so that they understand that the designation only applies if they demonstrate the objectives established in their development plans.

For the purposes of this chapter, we will focus primarily on understanding the idea of talent pools. Let's assume that a talent pool is created for the position of plant manager. The feeder positions for our plant manager role are the department heads in our manufacturing facilities. An implied concept here is that we are reaching down two levels below our target position to develop the talent for that position.

From this group, we identify candidates for our assistant plant manager position. The premise is that we would not select anyone for the assistant plant manager position who did not have the potential to become a plant manager. Another implied assumption is that there are no terminal assistant plant managers. The "owners" of this pool are likely the head of plant operations or maybe the president of the division. The current plant managers are part of this group, along with the people above them who are responsible for this pool.

There are a few things that need to happen among the senior people who "own" this pool. They need to abandon their plant focus and instead think about the greater needs of the organization. That means a plant manager can't protect or try to keep an assistant manager from being promoted. The other requirement is for the people supervising the pool to be candid and honest. If a plant manager has concerns or information about a department head that is being considered for the pool, it must be shared. This is not a popularity contest, but an assessment of a person's competence to do the job and his or her learning agility to handle unknown situations.

In our work at Burke Assessments, we've found that the people who have ownership for talent pools often are initially uncomfortable or unable to have these conversations with each other. It can take several years before they are ready to have and lead discussions about coworkers they may know well and consider friends. Human resources can play a big role in promoting this work. Concerns or issues about members of a talent pool and their capabilities should be encouraged and supported to keep discussions focused on the organization and its needs. People who participate in talent pool discussions are entitled to their opinions, but those opinions must be supported by examples and data. The decisions they will make are too important to be guided only by feelings and perceptions.

Done well, succession planning involves looking at something a person has done in the past and then trying to predict his or her ability to be successful in a different role in the future. Many organizations use something called a 9 Box to visualize this relationship between performance, or what someone has done in the past, and his or her future potential. Organizations use the 9 Box to visualize each candidate in the pool and whether the issues he or she needs to address are performance, potential or both.

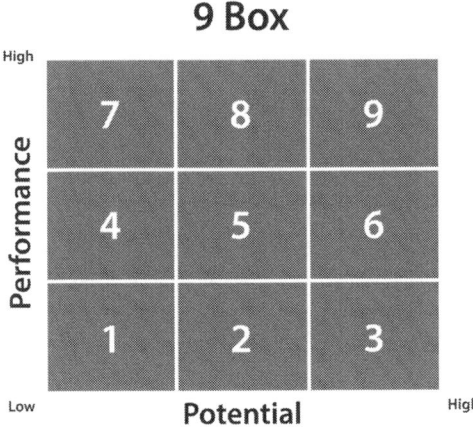

9 Box

The Y axis, or the performance side of the matrix, is straightforward. The person whose performance we are reviewing has done these jobs or had these experiences. We may debate the competencies that needed to be demonstrated to do that job. For more organizations, it is the x axis, or the potential side, that becomes more difficult to operationalize because it is unknown. This also is where learning agility becomes a consideration.

Many people working in talent management agree that a person's learning agility is one of the best predictors of leadership potential. With the *Burke Learning Agility Inventory Self-Assessment* to measure learning agility, we now have a way to measure leadership potential. For the purpose of talent pools, we are going to make a few assumptions. Our high-potential candidates in our plant manager talent pool have all been assessed using the *Burke Learning Agility Self-Assessment*. As part of this assessment, they have confirmed that the information about them in the assessment report is accurate.

Another assumption we'll make is that the owners of the talent pool have been trained as assessors. In a perfect situation, they would have experienced the assessment process themselves. At a minimum, they would have received training in how to use the learning agility dimensions and competencies for assessment and development purposes. As mentioned at the beginning of this chapter, training should include a consistent understanding and use of terms. For example, if one of the pool owners is using the term *Flexibility* from the *Burke Learning Agility Self-Assessment* to describe a strength or development need of a potential plant manager, then he or she is using the definition of *Flexibility* as "being open to new ideas and proposing new solutions." This process of using the definitions accurately takes time and practice; a typical group might spend one to two hours reviewing definitions and discussing why a behavior does or does not fit a learning agility dimension.

The same process is necessary when using competencies. Burke Assessments defines a competency with both a label and a one-line definition. A competency includes three to five behavioral descriptions, or indicators. If a person is demonstrating a competency, he or she is doing one or more of those behaviors, and each behavior should be specified. We believe that it's just as important to specify the behaviors that the person is not demonstrating, as this will focus and guide development discussions.

If talent pool owners do not receive training on learning agility and competency definitions, their discussions can become vague and risk being unproductive.

JOB / PERSON FIT

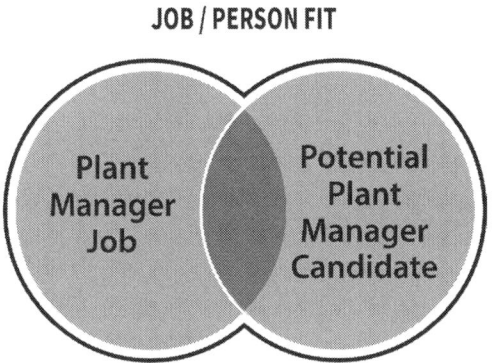

The nice thing about talent pool discussions is that regardless of who we are talking about, we are looking at the degree of "fit" between what a job requires and where a person is today. To help that person move forward, the next step that pool owners must focus on is identifying the experiences, projects or assignments the candidate needs for the pool owners to feel comfortable that he or she is "ready now." "Ready now" does not mean that the person possesses 100% of the qualities or skills a job requires. "Ready now" means there are no major deficiencies that would make the pool owners uncomfortable about putting a person in a specific job. Going back to our role as owners of the plant manager pool, we agree and accept that our strongest candidate for the role may be missing some of the elements required to succeed, but those will be outlined and included in his or her development plan for becoming a plant manager.

There is a term in talent management that was invented by Mike Lombardo and Bob Eichinger called "assignmentology" that they write about in their book *The Leadership Machine: Architecture to Develop Leaders for Any Future*. Assignmentology is an approach that can be used by human resources and line managers to determine the competencies and learning agility dimensions that are required to complete a job or project. Once the competencies and learning agility dimensions required to do a job are established, an organization can match jobs and assignments to employees based on their need to develop specific competencies or learning agility dimensions. The matching of person to role is targeted and intentional.

Part of talent management's role should be to support succession planning by determining competencies and learning agility dimensions needed for a particular assignment. The succession planners can then match people with roles or assignments based on the developmental opportunities the roles or assignments provide.

What follows is an assignment that can be given to a person in the plant manager talent pool to address specific development needs. In this case, it's for the fictional Megan, who is an assistant plant manager for a beverage company.

SAMPLE ASSIGNMENT FOR MEGAN JONES

This plant produces aluminum cans. From time to time, the cans are picking up an "off" taste during the production process. This taste is then being detected in either the beer or soft drinks that are put in the cans. When the "off" taste occurs in the production process, it usually remains for several days and over several shifts before it goes away. The problem is not identified until the quality assurance process, which happens after the cans are filled. Any product produced with an "off" taste must be dumped. The objective of this project is to isolate and eliminate this "off" taste.

Learning Agility Dimensions That Need to be Demonstrated on This Project:
- *Experimenting*
- *Collaborating*
- *Feedback Seeking*
- *Reflecting*

Competencies Required to Be Successful on This Project:
- Problem Solving
- Results Orientation
- Quality Focus
- Teamwork and Collaboration
- Risk Taking

Megan's Learning Agility Scores

Megan Jones – 2024-06-25 (GMT)

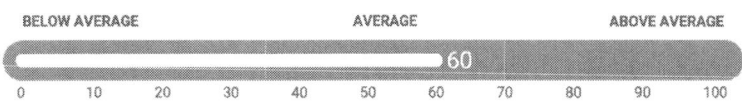

BELOW AVERAGE	AVERAGE	ABOVE AVERAGE

60

| 0 | 10 | 20 | 30 | 40 | 50 | 60 | 70 | 80 | 90 | 100 |

Overall Score Interpretation

Your score, at the 60th percentile, reflects a solid average score as compared to the norm (comparison) group indicated above. Compared with peers from this group, you display a good level of flexibility, skills, and motivation. Your capacity to apply agile behavior in learning situations is consistent, and with just a bit more focus, you can further enhance your agility and adaptability.

Subscale Scores

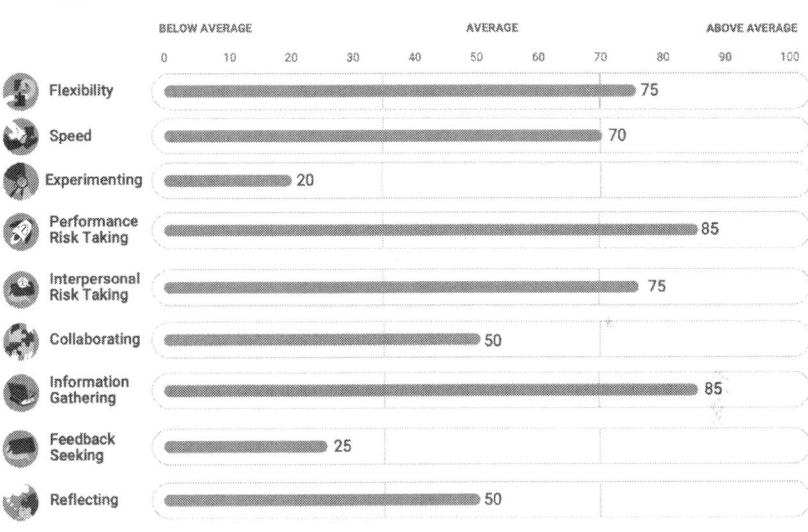

	BELOW AVERAGE	AVERAGE	ABOVE AVERAGE
Flexibility			75
Speed			70
Experimenting	20		
Performance Risk Taking			85
Interpersonal Risk Taking			75
Collaborating		50	
Information Gathering			85
Feedback Seeking	25		
Reflecting		50	

TOP 3 AREAS OF OPPORTUNITY	Raters' Average
Problem Solving Evaluates problems from different perspectives to determine most important issues.	2.2/5.0
Quality Focus Leads continued efforts that operate at the necessary pace to maximize success.	3.4/5.0
Risk Taking Recognizes critical interrelationships among key business variables.	2.6/5.0

Megan, our assistant plant manager who is given this assignment, is low on her *Burke Learning Agility Self-Assessment* results in **Experimenting** and **Feedback Seeking**, and medium on **Collaborating** and **Reflecting.** Her 360-degree feedback results show a need to improve in **Problem Solving, Quality Focus** and **Risk Taking.** Although the project also requires **Results Orientation** and **Teamwork and Collaboration**, Megan already possesses these skills. As her plant manager pool owners, we will discuss this information with her when she receives the assignment.

Before we go further with Megan, it's important to note that each person who is being developed in the talent pool needs to be "owned" by a specific member of the pool. Owning a person's development means providing support and direction from the project's beginning to end. Selecting the right person for this role is important. For example, while it might be convenient if a plant manager "owned" the assistant plant manager at the plant where they both currently worked. It may not be possible if an assistant plant manager is in one plant and the plant manager is in another. The most important issue is matching a plant manager with an assistant plant manager who gives the time and attention needed for development to occur.

Having people who are in different chains of command "own" a talent pool candidate can also help the development process, because it can be difficult for direct supervisors to be objective about the people who report to them. "Owning" a talent pool candidate means talking at least once a week with the candidate to understand how the effort is going, not to micromanage, but to understand what the candidate is learning.

The person who is assisting with the candidate's development should ask what is going well and not well with an assigned project, for example. The owner also should be talking with the person about competencies and learning agility dimensions that he or she is using, or ones that could be used.

At the next talent pool review, the owner will be expected to report on how well our candidate performed on his or her developmental assignment. The main objective of the review is to answer three questions:

- Did the person demonstrate the competencies and learning agility dimensions the assignment was intended to develop?
- How well did he or she do?
- What is the evidence that this person demonstrated these capabilities?

The discussion around the table among the other owners of this talent pool should be whether we are satisfied that Megan has demonstrated the capabilities defined by the group as important for a plant manager. If the answer is yes, then she is termed "ready now." Megan should be considered for the next opening that comes up for a plant manager, along with a slate of other "ready now" candidates. As openings for other critical jobs occur, they should be filled by the "ready now" people in our talent pool. This in turn creates openings in the pool.

As the owners of the pool, we should then trigger a mechanism to backfill openings in the pool. Openings in the pool can also occur because someone in the pool takes a job with another organization or does not do well in a development assignment. We can then take that person out of the pool and replace him or her with someone else. Alternatively, we can give a person we are unsure of another project to work on before we make a final determination about his or her potential.

In most companies, people who leave the talent pool because they do not accomplish their development plans can remain in their current roles. They would have a development plan like any other employee, but would no longer be considered "high potential." In the case of our assistant plant manager, the person would likely be encouraged to leave the organization or move into another position in the organization. Remember at the beginning of this process we said we did not want to put any assistant plant managers in the pool who did not have the potential to be a plant manager. Once we determine that a person has not successfully completed an assignment, and therefore is no longer being considered as a potential plant manager, we need to move him or her out of the assistant plant manager position. This would prevent us from having a "blocked" position, in the sense that a former high potential candidate was preventing other potential assistant plant manager candidates from assuming that role.

NOTE: The competencies discussed in Megan's scenario came from a list of generic behavioral competencies that Burke Assessments (formerly EASI•Consult) uses in selection projects.

CHAPTER 18

INTEGRATING THE *BURKE LEARNING AGILITY SELF-ASSESSMENT REPORT* WITH COACHING

Coaching is an approach in which one person works with another individual one-on-one to help improve his or her performance. Although this approach can be between a manager and his or her employee, such arrangements can feel awkward, as employees typically have a subordinate relationship with their managers. The only way that a boss can typically coach an employee is if he or she explains how coaching is different from normal interactions, which typically involves a boss giving assignments and an employee carrying them out. For a boss to be able to coach an employee effectively, the boss must explain to the person that he or she wants to have a "coaching" conversation. This signals the employee that the interaction is going to be different. Because of the inherent awkwardness in a boss coaching an employee, more traditional coaching engagements involve hiring a consultant from outside the organization to provide coaching. Some larger organizations have internal coaches that can be engaged in a coaching assignment in the same way an external coach is engaged. The compensation arrangement is different.

There are two basic approaches to coaching: directive and nondirective. Most performance coaching in organizations involves a nondirective approach, with the coach asking lots of questions of the person, but not giving many answers in return. This variation of the Socratic method is intentional and designed to help the employee think about what he or she is doing, and not doing, on the job. This type of reflection slows down the situation and can help the person be better prepared to handle situations in the future.

The other approach to coaching is a directive approach, in which a coach tells a person what to do and how to do it. This is more analogous to how coaches lead in sports. This type of coaching is effective, but only if used sparingly and in combination with a non-directive approach. A combination of directive and non-directive coaching ensures that the person being coached is reflecting and integrating the new things learned into his or her thought process.

Regardless of the approach taken, the objective of coaching is to address a capability or learning agility dimension that the person does not currently possess but will need for a specific job in the future. For that reason, it is important for both the coach and employee to be clear in understanding the issues that they are working to address. The organization can decide whether to tell the person the job he or she is being groomed for. However, the coach should know this information, as it will help him or her better focus efforts and energy. At Burke Assessments, our consultants typically work with organizations that have one or more people who have the potential to take on greater responsibilities, but not without additional and specific preparation. Our work usually includes helping these employees develop new skills or learning agility dimensions, or to correct blind spots in their development that they may not recognize or realize are important. As outsiders to the organizations that we work with, our coaches stress that employees should feel honored to be selected for this attention, and that they should approach coaching as an opportunity, not a punishment.

In our typical coaching engagements, the person being coached completes both a critical thinking and personality test. We also use the *Burke Learning Agility Inventory Self-Assessment* as an assessment for learning agility and interview the person's supervisor to understand his or her perspective. We might administer a 360-degree competency questionnaire to get input from the person who is being coached, as well as his or her boss, peers and subordinates. If a 360-degree competency tool is not used, we would request to interview some of the people who would have been asked to provide input on a 360-degree competency assessment.

All this information is then summarized into a report that addresses the employee's strengths and areas that need improvement. Our consultant first reviews the report with the employee and makes any revisions necessary to correct errors or inaccuracies. If all our findings are accurate and factual, no changes are made. Our consultant then arranges a meeting with the employee and his or her supervisor or the person who engaged Burke Assessments for the coaching assignment. Ideally, such meetings are led by the employee, and are mostly between the employee and the boss, with our coach supplying information as needed about the report and testing process. These meetings also give opportunities for the employee to share what he or she has learned from the report, which usually leads to an agreement between the supervisor, the employee, and the coach as to the objectives of the coaching engagement.

USING THE *BURKE LEARNING AGILITY INVENTORY SELF-ASSESSMENT REPORT* IN COACHING

Next, we will move the discussion to how we incorporate the *Burke Learning Agility Self-Assessment* into a coaching engagement. Here is a sample *Burke Learning Agility Self-Assessment* profile report for an individual that we'll use as an illustration.

Rhonda's Overall Learning Agility Self-Assessment Profile

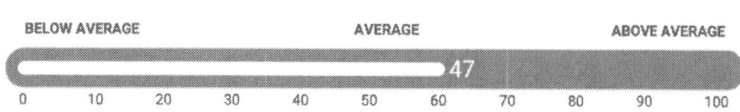

BELOW AVERAGE	AVERAGE	ABOVE AVERAGE

0   10   20   30   40   50   60   70   80   90   100

Overall Score Interpretation

Your score, at the 47th percentile, reflects a solid average score as compared to the norm (comparison) group indicated above. Compared with peers from this group, you display a good level of flexibility, skills, and motivation. Your capacity to apply agile behavior in learning situations is consistent, and with just a bit more focus, you can further enhance your agility and adaptability.

Subscale Scores

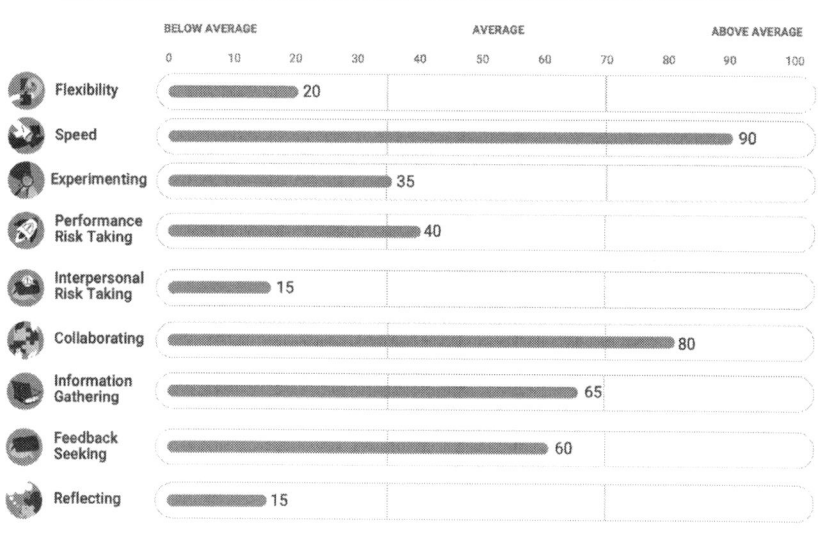

	Score
Flexibility	20
Speed	90
Experimenting	35
Performance Risk Taking	40
Interpersonal Risk Taking	15
Collaborating	80
Information Gathering	65
Feedback Seeking	60
Reflecting	15

The report is for a person who scored highest in the learning agility dimension of *Speed* and lowest on the learning agility dimensions of *Reflecting* and *Interpersonal Risk Taking*. The rest of the overall report describes an individual who is very bright and self-confident, but sometimes rushes to finish a project, and in doing so misses critical information. He also does not have much patience with subordinates who cannot absorb information as quickly as he can.

In this example, the coach is going to use the learning agility dimensions of *Reflecting* and *Interpersonal Risk Taking* to work on the objectives identified in the report and in the conversation with the employee's boss. Sometimes this is referred to as working "against the grain" (Lombardo, & Eichinger, 2000). The coach will help the employee use a learning agility approach that is not yet a capability. Research has shown that the more learning agility dimensions a person can access and use, the greater his or her potential will be in current and future jobs.

Burke Assessments' coaching engagements usually last for about six months. During this time, we typically hold weekly meetings with the employee for the first month, and then monthly meetings for the remainder of the engagement. In some instances, the employee wants to rehearse a specific situation with the coach before it occurs, and these meetings provide opportunities to discuss how to use a learning agility dimension that needs to be strengthened. After the employee experiences the situation for which he or she rehearsed, a debriefing session is held with the coach. These meetings also involve a discussion of what went well, what didn't go well, and what the employee could have done differently or better.

The debriefing also provides opportunities to discuss using the unfamiliar or uncomfortable learning agility dimension.

In addition to the regularly scheduled meetings, the employee, supervisor and coach may decide to hold an interim meeting. Usually, there is also a final meeting with the employee, supervisor and coach to discuss the objectives of the coaching assignment and whether they were accomplished. This is the time for the supervisor to share and comment on observations made during the coaching period. The employee should lead the discussion with his or her supervisor and coach, and share what was learned. The coach should add his or her perspective, and talk about the progress that has been made, areas that still need improvement, and opportunities in the work environment that could be made available to the employee to address those areas. As the coaching process comes to an end, the idea is to phase the coach out and integrate the employee's development and learning agility needs into the overall work environment.

In the next and final chapter, we'll shift our focus from individual to organizational development.

CHAPTER 19

USING THE *BURKE LEARNING AGILITY INVENTORY SELF-ASSESSMENT REPORT* AS AN ORGANIZATIONAL DEVELOPMENT INTERVENTION

In the previous chapters, we looked at various ways to use the *Burke Learning Agility Self-Assessment* as a tool to assist individuals. In some cases, such as training and performance management, the tools were used with groups of people, but the focus was on the individual. In this chapter, we will show how to use the *Burke Learning Agility Self-Assessment* to help two or more individuals work together more effectively.

In Example 1, we will use *Burke Learning Agility Self-Assessment* data for both a boss and his subordinate to examine where they might naturally work well together, and where their learning agility profiles might indicate tension between them.

In Example 2, we will look at *Burke Learning Agility Self-Assessment* data for a boss, who is the manager of a financial services team, as well as composite information for his team. We will use both sets of *Burke Learning Agility Self-Assessment* information to uncover areas of strength and opportunity for both the manager and his team. We'll also outline ways they can improve specific dimensions to better serve their organization's customers.

Example 3 shows how the *Burke Learning Agility Self-Assessment* can be used with an organization's own competency questionnaire tool to provide much richer information about what a manager can do to be more effective. We'll also explain how the manager can use the information to improve performance across his organization.

Example 4 includes both *Burke Learning Agility Inventory Self-Assessment* and Hogan Personality Inventory data for a director of finance and shows how he and his boss can use the information to work together more effectively.

The final scenario, Example 5 will include composite *Burke Learning Agility Inventory Self-Assessment* data for an organization to examine the strengths and challenges it faces institutionally. We will then drill down and look at a composite for several functional groups within this organization to focus on the challenges each function will have, particularly as they try to coexist within the larger organization.

EXAMPLE 1: SALESPERSON AND SALES MANAGER

The boss in this scenario is Mark, a sales manager who has worked for the same consumer products company for 20 years. He has covered his current sales territory for seven years, and is considered to be a good developer of salespeople. One of his subordinates is Jessica, a salesperson who has been with the company for just over two years. Jessica was hired to work for the company right out of college and is seen as someone with a lot of potential. Immediately after joining the company, she spends six months in an early career program, which gives her exposure to different functions in the company. She then works as an executive assistant to one of the regional vice presidents of sales for six months, a role in which she has no specific customer responsibility.

After completing her first year with the company, Jessica is moved to a different region and is now working for Mark. In the company, Jessica is viewed very much as a typical, young, go-getter salesperson, and is responsible for 200 accounts.

Both Jessica and Mark attend a seminar where they take and receive feedback on the *Burke Learning Agility Self-Assessment*. Their profiles appear next. First, we'll summarize the strengths and developmental areas for Jessica, then Mark. Then we'll look at where their profiles match up and are different, and how that will affect their ability to work together.

Jessica's Overall Learning Agility Self-Assessment Profile

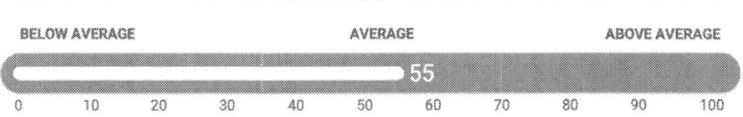

Overall Score Interpretation

Your score, at the 55th percentile, reflects a solid average score as compared to the norm (comparison) group indicated above. Compared with peers from this group, you display a good level of flexibility, skills, and motivation. Your capacity to apply agile behavior in learning situations is consistent, and with just a bit more focus, you can further enhance your agility and adaptability.

Subscale Scores

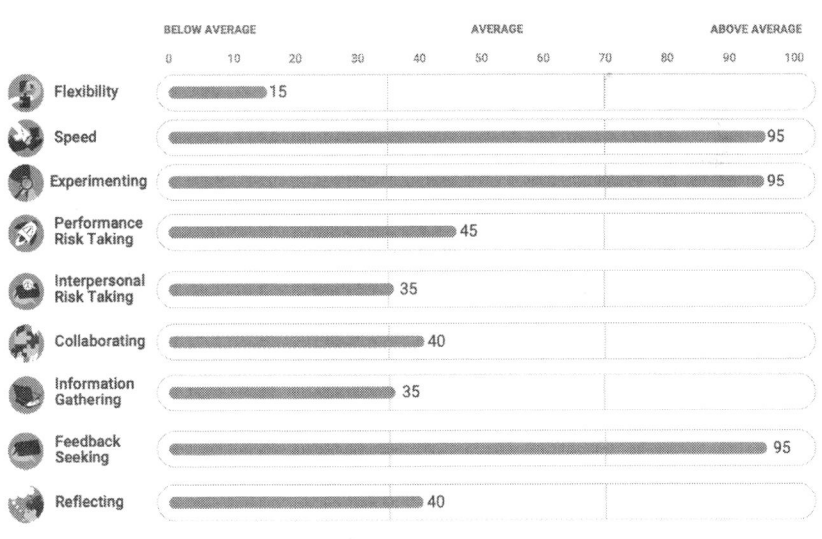

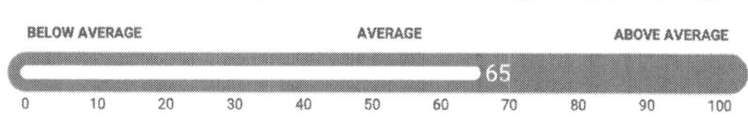

Mark's Overall Learning Agility Self-Assessment Profile

BELOW AVERAGE	AVERAGE	ABOVE AVERAGE

65

0   10   20   30   40   50   60   70   80   90   100

Overall Score Interpretation

Your score, at the 65th percentile, reflects a solid average score as compared to the norm (comparison) group indicated above. Compared with peers from this group, you display a good level of flexibility, skills, and motivation. Your capacity to apply agile behavior in learning situations is consistent, and with just a bit more focus, you can further enhance your agility and adaptability.

Subscale Scores

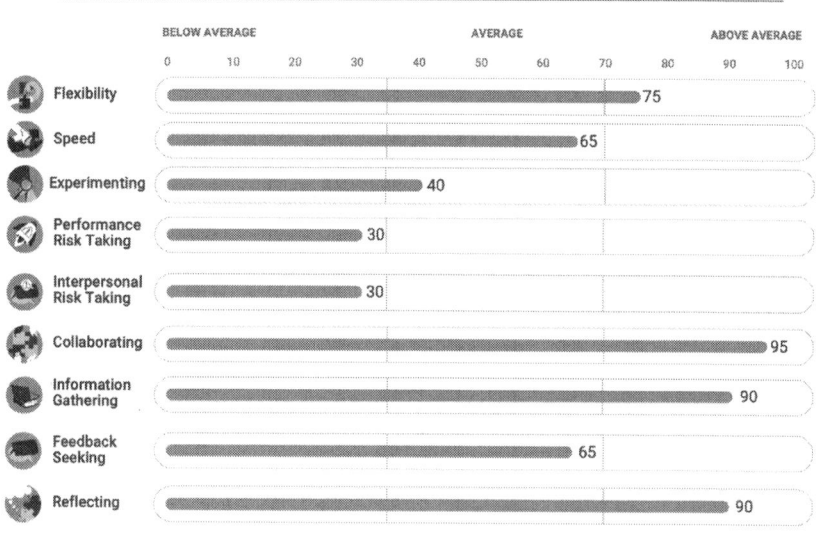

	BELOW AVERAGE	AVERAGE	ABOVE AVERAGE
Flexibility			75
Speed			65
Experimenting		40	
Performance Risk Taking		30	
Interpersonal Risk Taking		30	
Collaborating			95
Information Gathering			90
Feedback Seeking			65
Reflecting			90

Jessica's learning agility strengths, which are her highest scores and those above the 70th percentile are *Flexibility, Speed, Experimenting* and *Feedback Seeking*. Her development areas, which are her lowest scores and those below the 50th percentile, are *Performance Risk Taking, Interpersonal Risk Taking, Collaborating, Information Gathering* and *Reflecting*.

Mark's learning agility strengths are *Flexibility, Collaborating, Information Gathering* and *Reflecting*. His lowest learning agility areas are *Experimenting, Performance Risk Taking* and *Interpersonal Risk Taking*. The dimensions of *Speed* and *Feedback Seeking* are assets, or things Mark can draw on, but not his strongest capabilities. We determine this because these are learning agility dimensions in the intermediate or 35th to 70th percentile range.

An area where Jessica and Mark share strength is *Flexibility*. They are both open to new ideas and to proposing new solutions. They should use that common strength in their work together. Neither Mark nor Jessica is strong in the areas of *Performance Risk Taking* and *Interpersonal Risk Taking*. This may make some of their discussions about areas for improvement more difficult. Neither individual is comfortable talking about conflict, and they are unlikely to push each other to try new ways of interacting. In a coaching situation, we would point out to them that Jessica is high in *Feedback Seeking*, which means she is open to it, as you would hope she would be early in her career. With a score in the 68th percentile, *Feedback Seeking* is an area where Mark has the capability, although it is not his strongest learning agility area. The important thing is that he can access this ability.

With this information, Mark might want to think about presenting feedback to Jessica as an attempt at collaborating with her, which is clearly one of his strengths. Although "salesperson" is an individual contributor role, Jessica needs to understand and develop her *Collaborating* dimension. An example for her would be *Collaborating* to find new ways to partner with clients to grow sales. Even more important, she will need to develop her *Collaborating* dimension in preparation for future roles with the company that will require her to manage the work of others.

Mark also has a learning agility strength in *Reflecting*, a capability we would hope that someone supervising the work of others would have. While Mark doesn't want to stifle Jessica's enthusiasm to do things quickly (*Speed*), Mark should coach Jessica to ensure that she uses *Speed* with *Reflecting*, which will help prevent her from making the same mistakes over and over. Mark and Jessica should have a long and prosperous working relationship if they continue to use the *Burke Learning Agility Inventory Self-Assessment* data as a diagnostic tool to help them have the kinds of conversations they will need to have to learn and grow in their careers.

EXAMPLE 2: MANAGER AND HIS FINANCIAL SERVICES TEAM

The financial services team at a midsize regional financial institution includes Claude, a manager; two analysts; and an administrative support person. The team has been working together for just over a year and provides wealth management, capital markets, and asset management support for individuals and families. Claude has been with the organization for 15 years. He has hired and built the team, but members of the group feel they could work together more effectively. The analysts want to learn additional technical and "soft" skills that would allow them to interchangeably serve the group's customers. The team's administrative person is very bright and wants to do more to contribute to the team's success.

Claude's Overall Learning Agility Self-Assessment Profile

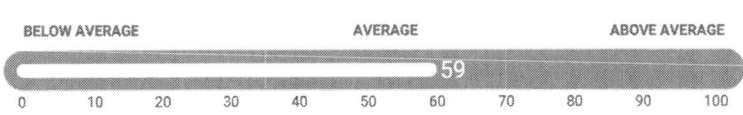

Overall Score Interpretation

Your score, at the 59th percentile, reflects a solid average score as compared to the norm (comparison) group indicated above. Compared with peers from this group, you display a good level of flexibility, skills, and motivation. Your capacity to apply agile behavior in learning situations is consistent, and with just a bit more focus, you can further enhance your agility and adaptability.

Subscale Scores

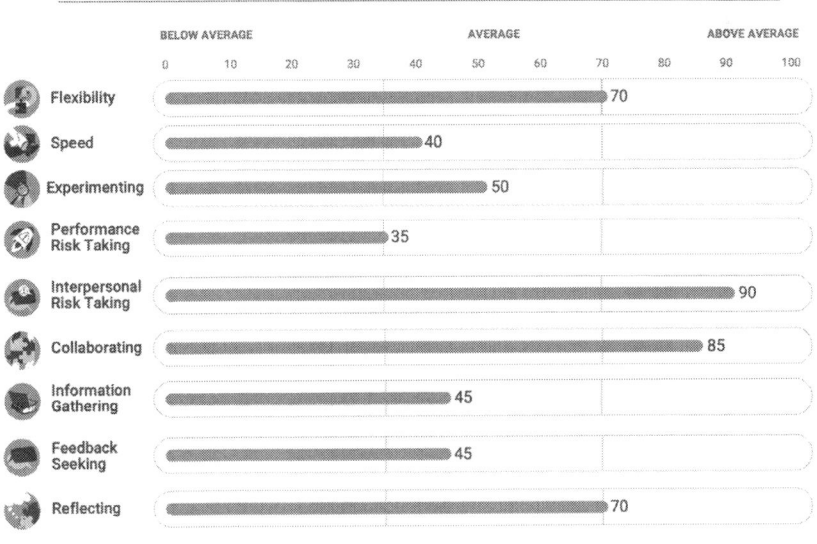

CLAUDE – TEAM MANAGER

Claude's *Burke Learning Agility Self-Assessment* overall score at the 59th percentile would put him in average range on the assessment, which has been normed with, or compared to, other mid-level and upper-level managers. This score tells us that Claude demonstrates learning agility, but not at a high level.

Claude's highest dimensions (above the 70th percentile) are *Interpersonal Risk Taking* and *Collaborating*, followed by *Reflecting* and *Flexibility*. From this information, we know that he is capable of talking with his team about how they are perceived by customers or other team members. His *Collaborating* score says he can work well with his team. His *Flexibility* score says he is open to new ideas, and the *Reflecting* score says he can step back after an event and think about what went well and how his team can improve.

Claude may have greater difficulty with *Speed, Performance Risk Taking, Information Gathering* and *Feedback Seeking*. We know this because his scores on these dimensions are lower than the 50th percentile. In fact, Claude must push himself to try new behaviors quickly. He is not inclined to seek new activities to challenge himself, and he doesn't tend to ask others for feedback on his ideas (*Feedback Seeking*) or the team's overall performance. He also does not tend to collect information (*Information Gathering*) to stay current in his field.

Experimenting, at the 50th percentile, is something Claude can access to try new things, but is not a dimension that he is strong at currently. In summary, Claude is open and good to work with. He can reflect on issues that come up at work, and talk to his team about how he interacts with them and how they interact with each other. He is not a quick study (*Speed*), does not take performance risks, (*Performance Risk Taking*), does not collect a lot of information (*Information Gathering*), and does not seek feedback from others (*Feedback Seeking*).

Team's Overall Learning Agility

Note: The percentile score by dimension are based on
averaging each of individual's scores for that dimension.

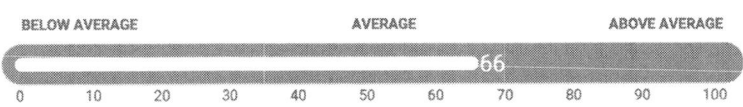

BELOW AVERAGE	AVERAGE	ABOVE AVERAGE

66

0   10   20   30   40   50   60   70   80   90   100

Overall Score Interpretation

Your score, at the 66th percentile, reflects a solid average score as compared to the norm (comparison) group indicated above. Compared with peers from this group, you display a good level of flexibility, skills, and motivation. Your capacity to apply agile behavior in learning situations is consistent, and with just a bit more focus, you can further enhance your agility and adaptability.

Subscale Scores

	BELOW AVERAGE	AVERAGE	ABOVE AVERAGE
	0 10 20 30	40 50 60 70	80 90 100
Flexibility		65	
Speed		68	
Experimenting			80
Performance Risk Taking		60	
Interpersonal Risk Taking		70	
Collaborating		75	
Information Gathering		75	
Feedback Seeking	40		
Reflecting		60	

CLAUDE'S TEAM

The *Burke Learning Agility Self-Assessment* composite score for Claude's team is at the 66th percentile. This puts them in the high end of the average range. The test is normed based on other mid-level and upper-level managers. It shows us that the overall learning agility of Claude's team is higher than for Claude himself, which is a positive for the team.

The overall learning agility strengths of Claude's team (at the 66th percentile) are *Experimenting, Interpersonal Risk Taking, Collaborating* and *Information Gathering.* The weakest learning agility dimension, below the 50th percentile, is *Feedback Seeking.* There also are other learning agility dimensions that the team can access that are above the 50th percentile, but below the 70th percentile. Those are *Flexibility, Speed, Performance Risk Taking* and *Reflecting.*

Claude's team is willing to try new behaviors (*Experimenting*) and to talk about how they are working together. The team members want to work together (*Collaborating*) and stay current in their areas of expertise (*Information Gathering*).

THE PLAN FORWARD

In this scenario, Burke Assessments has facilitated a few meetings with Claude and his team to share both sets of *Burke Learning Agility Self-Assessment* data. In one of those meetings, the team reflects on a project it recently completed, including what went well and what they could have done differently (*Reflecting* and *Feedback Seeking*). In the future, the group plans to hold a series of customer meetings and to look for other ways that its two analysts can share their expertise with customers. The team agrees that the meetings will require *Experimenting* and *Performance Risk Taking*, and that the analysts will need to do *Information Gathering* before the meetings. *Collaborating* also will be required to ensure the two analysts do not duplicate their efforts.

The team intentionally decides to try some new approaches to these customer meetings (*Flexibility, Experimenting* and *Performance Risk Taking*). After the meetings are held, another session is scheduled to look at what went well, not so well, and could be done differently in the future (*Reflecting* and *Feedback Seeking*).

By the end of the meeting, Claude is very aware that his analysts need him to be comfortable with what they plan to do, before they do it (*Performance Risk Taking*). He also knows he needs to delegate more to them if they are going to help grow the team's customer base (*Flexibility*). For his team to become more learning agile, Claude must encourage them to be intentional about looking at situations and applying the learning agility dimensions. He and his team also need to make learning agility a part of how they do their work.

EXAMPLE 3: HOSPITAL SENIOR MANAGER – *BURKE LEARNING AGILITY SELF-ASSESSMENT REPORT/*COMPETENCY DATA

Arne is the senior administrator for Acme Regional Medical Center, which is one of 10 hospitals in a larger health care system. When Acme was acquired by the system three years ago, Arne was named senior manager to accelerate Acme's ability to adopt the regional organization's systems and processes. The Acme health care system is trying to accelerate its senior managers' abilities to manage change, and recently offered Arne the opportunity to attend a leadership program in which he received feedback about his ability to demonstrate specific change skills. The measurements used during the program were the Acme Regional Competency Questionnaire (ARCQ) and the *Burke Learning Agility Inventory Self-Assessment.*

Arne's Overall Learning Agility Self-Assessment Profile

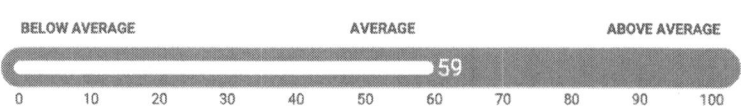

BELOW AVERAGE	AVERAGE	ABOVE AVERAGE

59

| 0 | 10 | 20 | 30 | 40 | 50 | 60 | 70 | 80 | 90 | 100 |

Overall Score Interpretation

Your score, at the 59th percentile, reflects a solid average score as compared to the norm (comparison) group indicated above. Compared with peers from this group, you display a good level of flexibility, skills, and motivation. Your capacity to apply agile behavior in learning situations is consistent, and with just a bit more focus, you can further enhance your agility and adaptability.

Subscale Scores

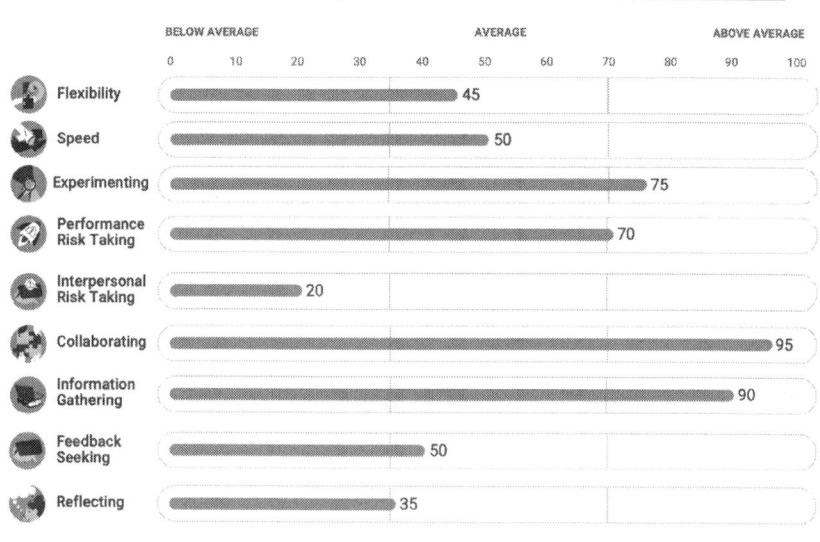

	BELOW AVERAGE	AVERAGE	ABOVE AVERAGE
Flexibility	45		
Speed	50		
Experimenting	75		
Performance Risk Taking	70		
Interpersonal Risk Taking	20		
Collaborating	95		
Information Gathering	90		
Feedback Seeking	50		
Reflecting	35		

BURKE LEARNING AGILITY SELF-ASSESSMENT DATA

Arne has learning agility strengths in the areas of *Experimenting, Performance Risk Taking, Collaborating* and *Information Gathering*; his scores on each of these dimensions are above the 70th percentile. He needs to strengthen his *Flexibility, Interpersonal Risk Taking* and *Reflecting,* which are all below the 50th percentile.

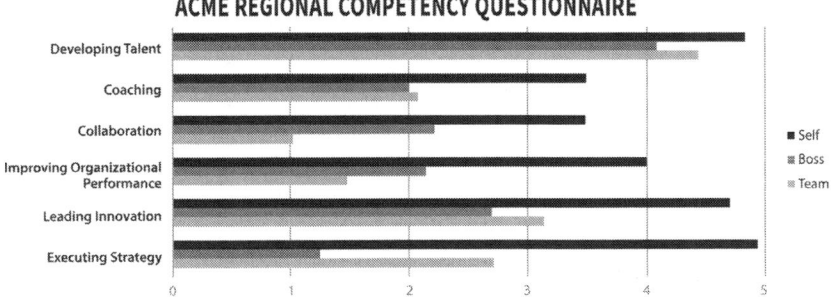

ACME REGIONAL COMPETENCY QUESTIONNAIRE DATA

The health care system's leadership views Arne as being good at Developing Talent. However, the system's executive leadership wants him to strengthen his skills in the areas of Leading Innovation, Executing Strategy, Improving Organizational Performance , Collaboration, and Coaching. These are areas where his perception and others' perceptions of him differ by more than one point.

> **Definition of the Acme Competencies**
> • **Developing Talent** - Takes steps to help others develop their skills and maximize their potential.
> • **Coaching** - Draws upon various learning techniques to continuously enhance others' overall effectiveness.
> • **Collaboration** - Develops and maintains effective team relationships and performance.
> • **Improving Organizational Performance** - Ensures that tasks, initiatives, goals and business objectives are met.
> • **Leading Innovation** - Actively seeks out new and creative ideas and opportunities.
> • **Executing Strategy** - Understands environmental trends and looks at organizational strengths and weaknesses and how they impact the organization's overall priorities.

The data presented here suggests that Arne should be good at thinking about information and collecting information from sources inside and outside Acme. In the future, while he is collecting information (*Information Gathering*, a strength), Arne should also seek feedback (*Feedback Seeking*, a capability he can access, given his score is in the middle range). Being able to access a skill does not mean it will be facile to use. This is why if he can bring in other support when seeking feedback, he will be more likely to be successful in his efforts. This approach also will provide opportunities for him to grow in one of his weaker dimensions (***Interpersonal Risk Taking***, a dimension he needs to improve).

This data also shows us that Arne likes to take on new activities that challenge him, but struggles to act on ideas quickly (***Speed***). One suggestion to improve in these areas is to look at ARCQ data for patient and employee satisfaction to pinpoint ways to improve in these areas. This effort should include setting goals for himself that will directly affect his group's performance in these areas. In addition, Arne should use opportunities for ***Information Gathering*** and ***Feedback Seeking*** to identify people who can teach him how to better collaborate with and coach his employees. Although he is believed to be a good developer of talent, he may need to do so in a more directive way that requires him to seek feedback. If Arne gets some tips from others about Coaching and ***Collaborating***, he may be able to identify opportunities to improve his organization's performance in a more lasting way.

EXAMPLE 4: DIRECTOR AND VICE PRESIDENT OF FINANCE

In this scenario, Burke Assessments is researching the relationship between learning agility and personality. It is believed there is a relationship between the two constructs, and data is needed to support that hypothesis.

We soon have an opportunity to study this issue in greater detail when we are asked to work with Raul, the director of finance in the financial services division of a mortgage company. Raul has been with the company for five years and was recently promoted to the director role. His supervisor in his new role is Audrey, the vice president of finance for the division. Audrey has been with the organization for 20 years, and has seen it grow threefold in that time. She also was instrumental in building some of the systems and tools currently used in the finance area.

As Raul's supervisor, Audrey is fortunate to have access to his *Burke Learning Agility Inventory Self-Assessment* and Hogan Personality Inventory (HPI) reports. The information was collected as part of an assessment for selection that led to Raul's appointment as director of finance. Raul initially was one of three candidates for the position; the other two people were internal candidates. At the end of the process, Raul was the person determined to be the best fit for the job.

We'll show how Audrey can use information about Raul collected in his *Burke Learning Agility Self-Assessment* and HPI reports to help him succeed in his new role.

> **The definitions of the seven dimensions measured by the Hogan Personality Inventory are as follows:**
> • **Adjustment** - measures stress-tolerance, resilience, optimism and composure
> • **Ambition** - measures competitive drive, perceived energy and goal-orientation
> • **Sociability** - measures social energy, communication frequency and relationship-building
> • **Interpersonal Sensitivity** - measures tact, communication style and relationship-maintenance skill
> • **Prudence** - measures detail-orientation, organizational skills and dependability
> • **Inquisitive** - measures idea-orientation, level of curiosity and openness to new ideas
> • **Learning Approach** - measures learning style and propensity to seek new information and stay up to date

We will start by summarizing Raul's *Burke Learning Agility Self-Assessment* data and looking for dimensions that Audrey can leverage as she works with Raul. We also will identify learning agility dimensions that Raul might find more difficult to demonstrate. Next, we will layer the *Burke Learning Agility Self-Assessment* on to Raul's Hogan Personality Inventory data. This will give us information at the personality level as to things that will be easy or difficult for Raul to change.

Integrating the *Burke Learning Agility Inventory Self-Assessment* and the HPI data gives us a fuller and more in-depth picture of how to better work with Raul.

Raul's Overall Learning Agility Self-Assessment Profile

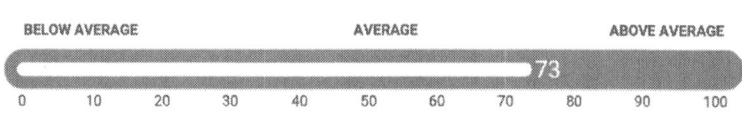

BELOW AVERAGE				AVERAGE				ABOVE AVERAGE	

73

0   10   20   30   40   50   60   70   80   90   100

Overall Score Interpretation

Your score, at the 73rd percentile, reflects a solid average score as compared to the norm (comparison) group indicated above. Compared with peers from this group, you display a good level of flexibility, skills, and motivation. Your capacity to apply agile behavior in learning situations is consistent, and with just a bit more focus, you can further enhance your agility and adaptability.

Subscale Scores

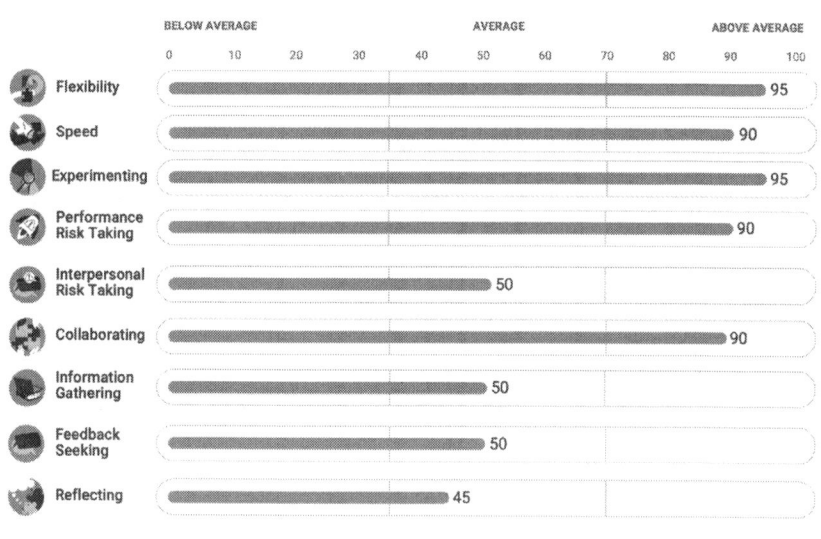

	BELOW AVERAGE				AVERAGE				ABOVE AVERAGE	
	0 10 20	30	40	50	60	70	80	90	100
Flexibility									95
Speed									90
Experimenting									95
Performance Risk Taking									90
Interpersonal Risk Taking				50					
Collaborating									90
Information Gathering				50					
Feedback Seeking				50					
Reflecting				45					

EXAMINATION OF *BURKE LEARNING AGILITY SELF-ASSESSMENT REPORT* DATA

Raul's learning agility strengths—those with scores above the 70th percentile—are *Flexibility, Speed, Experimenting, Performance Risk Taking* and *Collaborating*. Raul's learning agility developmental areas, or those with scores at or below the 50th percentile, are *Interpersonal Risk Taking, Information Gathering, Feedback Seeking* and *Reflecting*.

RAUL'S HPI PROFILE

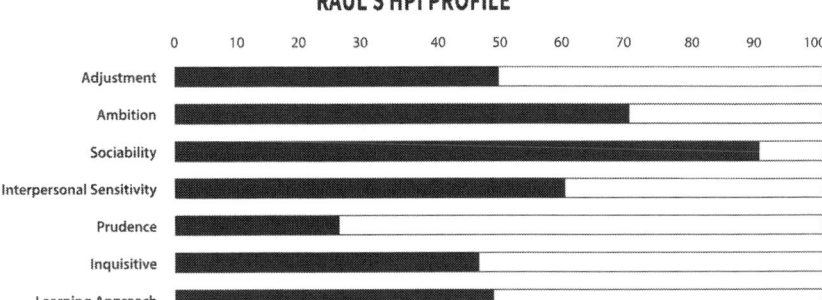

EXAMINATION OF HPI DATA

Raul is highly ambitious, has highly developed communication skills, and is good at building and maintaining relationships. He is not highly detail oriented or inquisitive, and is not likely to gather information on his own to grow in his personal knowledge.

IMPLICATIONS FOR MANAGING RAUL

The combination of the *Burke Learning Agility Inventory Self-Assessment* and Hogan data gives us some powerful information that can help Audrey as Raul's manager. By understanding how he tends to approach his work, she can help him leverage his strengths and work tendencies, as well as close gaps in learning agility dimensions. Here are a few examples:

> **Capitalizing on Strengths.** Audrey should help Raul capitalize on his learning agility strengths, which are *Flexibility, Speed, Experimenting, Performance Risk Taking* and *Collaborating*. In doing so, she can encourage him to use strong aspects of his personality that align with his learning agility. Let's start with where his personality characteristics line up with his learning agility strengths:

- Raul's HPI data indicates that he likely has strong communication skills (based on his strong interpersonal sensitivity and sociability) and that he is comfortable with building and maintaining relationships. A learning agility strength for him is *Collaborating*. We would expect Raul to easily build a strong team and establish relationships with his boss, his peers and his customers—relationships that will help him be successful in his job. We should also note that *Interpersonal Risk Taking* in Raul's learning agility profile was low, but we will return to this later.

- Raul's HPI data also indicates that he is ambitious. It is always easier for a supervisor like Audrey to help Raul tone that trait down, if necessary, than it would be to increase his ambition. Raul's learning agility strengths of *Experimenting* and *Performance Risk Taking* could be combined with his Ambition in ways that allow him to accomplish very positive things in his new role.

- There are a few concerns that emerge from Raul's HPI and learning agility information that he and Audrey will need to manage. Raul's HPI report shows a lower score on the Learning Approach; this is consistent with his low score on *Information Gathering* on the *Burke Learning Agility Self-Assessment*. He may need to find someone on his team who he can rely on to assume this responsibility. If Raul wants to work on this area, it could be built into an assignment he receives. This will likely never be something that becomes a strength for Raul. He will have to work hard to handle *Information Gathering* himself or delegate it to someone else.

- Two other aspects of Raul's personality are that he is not detail oriented or Inquisitive. This shows up in his learning agility profile as a low score on *Feedback Seeking*. Again these are things than can be worked on and should be included in a development plan. Raul will need to be very deliberate in seeking feedback from others. He may need the assistance of other people in his group to attend to detail and to make sure he is seeking feedback.

- Now let's return to the *Interpersonal Risk Taking* mentioned at the beginning of this section. This was one of Raul's lowest learning agility scores. This is a bit surprising given his strong Interpersonal Sensitivity and relationship-building skills. It may be that he has never needed to take interpersonal risks. However, he can be taught the behaviors needed to do this from the questions in the *Burke Learning Agility Self-Assessment* survey; a low score on a question can prompt opportunities to assign specific tasks that can help an individual improve in a weak dimension. It will be important for Raul to be intentional in trying these behaviors out and asking for feedback on how effective he is. Remember, *Feedback Seeking* is not one of his strengths.

- We have not yet addressed Raul's learning agility strengths of *Flexibility* and *Speed*. Audrey can help him understand that these are both important aspects of learning agility and he is fortunate to have these capabilities. Raul needs to appreciate that *Speed* can be the enemy of attention to detail, one of the areas in which he needs to improve. *Flexibility*, or the ability to adjust your perspective, is very valuable for a manager. *Reflecting* also came out as a development need for Raul on his *Burke Learning Agility Self-Assessment*. He can certainly build time for *Reflecting* into his planning before a project begins and at its end. He and Audrey also can add opportunities for *Reflecting* into their interactions.

As discussed in this example of Raul and Audrey, organizations can layer personality data on top of learning agility data to gain a more comprehensive picture of an individual's tendencies, capabilities and likely behaviors. This allows leaders, like Audrey, to adjust their leadership style to better understand and meet the needs of an individual employee.

EXAMPLE 5: ORGANIZATION – COMPOSITE BURKE LEARNING AGILITY INVENTORY SELF-ASSESSMENT REPORT

In this last scenario, we have *Burke Learning Agility Self-Assessment* data on an entire organization, Performax. With 500 employees, Performax is a medium-sized specialty manufacturing company that distributes its products nationally. The company's longevity and the experience it has gained have served as a barrier to entry for potential competitors. However, in recent years, several new entrants to the field have begun to take some of Performax's market share. This was why Performax became interested in the *Burke Learning Agility Self-Assessment*. The son of the company's president suggests that the *Burke Learning Agility Self-Assessment* might help the company's leadership better identify the organization's strengths and opportunities for improvement. What follows is a group profile for Performax.

Performax Organizational Composite Overall Scores
n = 500

Note: The percentile score by dimension represent the average
of all the respondents scores described as a percentage for each dimension.

BELOW AVERAGE	AVERAGE	ABOVE AVERAGE

56

0	10	20	30	40	50	60	70	80	90	100

Overall Score Interpretation

Your score, at the 56th percentile, reflects a solid average score as compared to the norm (comparison) group indicated above. Compared with peers from this group, you display a good level of flexibility, skills, and motivation. Your capacity to apply agile behavior in learning situations is consistent, and with just a bit more focus, you can further enhance your agility and adaptability.

Subscale Scores

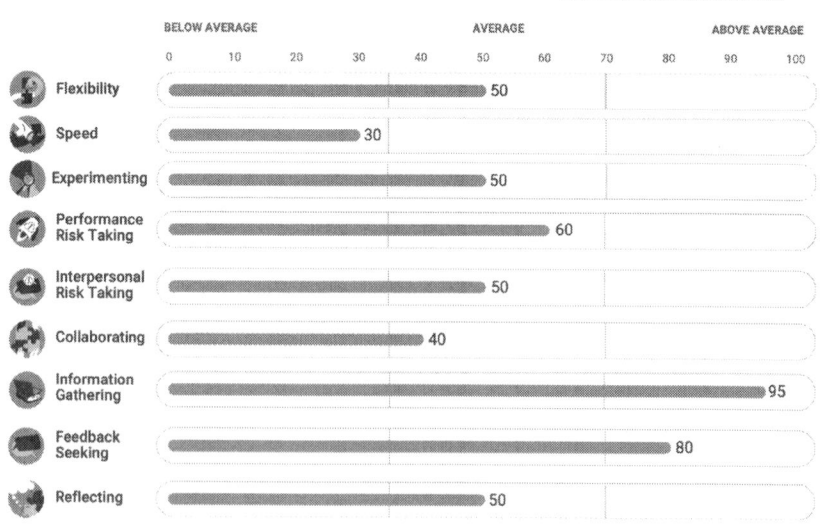

	BELOW AVERAGE			AVERAGE			ABOVE AVERAGE		
	0	10	20	30	40	50	60	70	80	90	100
Flexibility						50				
Speed				30						
Experimenting						50				
Performance Risk Taking							60			
Interpersonal Risk Taking						50				
Collaborating					40					
Information Gathering										95
Feedback Seeking									80	
Reflecting						50				

Looking at this composite data, we can tell that the organization is good at gathering information (*Information Gathering* and *Feedback Seeking*) about internal operations. Both of these dimensions are above the 70th percentile. From working with this company, we know it collects a large volume of data on performance, which is shared with employees at weekly, quarterly and annual meetings. It is not surprising that *Feedback Seeking* is so high on the *Burke Learning Agility Self-Assessment* composite. Because the data is fed back and used as a baseline to set new and higher goals, we expected *Performance Risk Taking* would be an organizational strength. There is a medium amount of ability to reflect on performance (*Reflecting*). The reaction when the data is presented is that this might be more true in some areas of the organization than others. There also is some willingness to consider new ideas (*Flexibility*). The thought is that this might be more specific to certain functions than others.

The learning agility dimensions where there is room for improvement are in working together across the organization (*Collaborating*), not acting on new ideas quickly (*Speed*) and not being candid with each other when issues arise (*Interpersonal Risk Taking*). All of these dimensions are below the 50th percentile.

The composite result gives the organization some things they can begin to work on immediately. The organization's senior leaders agree to create three task forces to address performance areas and learning agility dimensions that need improvement. xYz Consulting is asked to go back and aggregate the data by function. This request is itself an example of *Information Gathering* and *Feedback Seeking*.

Performax also asks xYz Consulting to create *Burke Learning Agility Self-Assessment* composites for three sub-groups in the organization. Their biggest concentrations of employees are in the categories of operations, with 300 people; sales and marketing, with 125 people; and staff, with 75 people. The operations group includes employees who work in and support manufacturing, including engineers. The sales and marketing group consists of all the customer-facing salespeople and the marketing team, which develops collateral materials to support sales. The staff group is a combination of human resources, legal, information technology and finance.

By breaking Performax's overall composite into three separate sub-groups, we were able to examine information that was somewhat different than what appeared in the organizational composite.

Operations Organizational Composite Overall Scores
n = 300

Note: The percentile score by dimension represent the average
of all the respondents scores described as a percentage for each dimension.

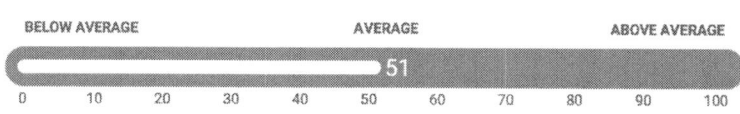

Overall Score Interpretation

Your score, at the 51st percentile, reflects a solid average score as compared to the norm (comparison) group indicated above. Compared with peers from this group, you display a good level of flexibility, skills, and motivation. Your capacity to apply agile behavior in learning situations is consistent, and with just a bit more focus, you can further enhance your agility and adaptability.

Subscale Scores

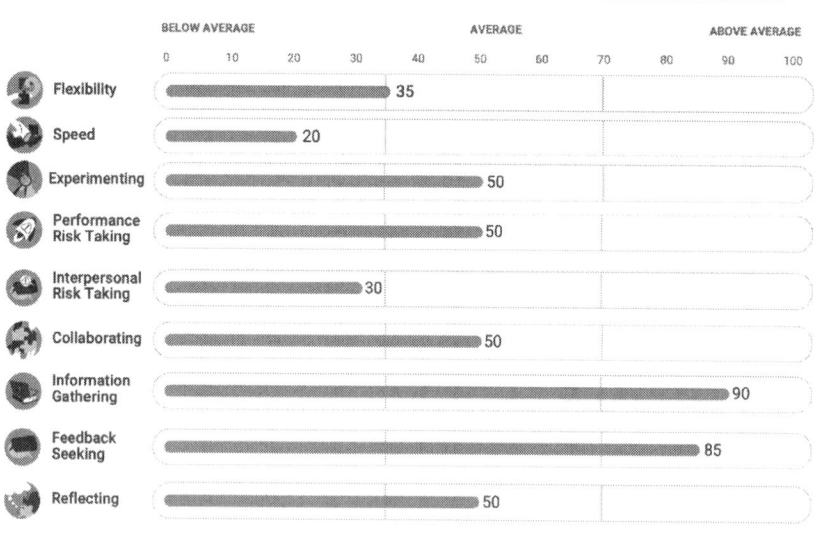

One thing we notice right away is that *Flexibility* is lower in operations than in the overall organization. This is common in a high-speed operations environment, where standardization is valued. *Speed* is a little lower in operations than in the overall organization. Changes in operations should be planned and probably tested on a small scale before being adopted across the manufacturing environment.

Collaborating is a little higher in operations than in the overall organization. About a year ago, the organization's manufacturing facility implemented a large cross-training program that was intended to give management more latitude in staffing. The managers have noticed that employees seem to be working better across jobs and functions, which is showing up in this learning agility dimension. The last area worth pointing out is *Interpersonal Risk Taking*, which is a little lower in operations than in the overall organization. That information paints a different picture than we were seeing with *Collaborating*. Digging deeper, we determine that while people feel comfortable *Collaborating* on production issues, *Collaborating* does not carry over to issues that are interpersonal.

Sales and Marketing Composite Overall Scores
n = 125

Note: The percentile score by dimension represent the average
of all the respondents scores described as a percentage for each dimension.

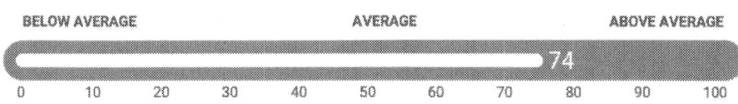

BELOW AVERAGE	AVERAGE	ABOVE AVERAGE

74

0   10   20   30   40   50   60   70   80   90   100

Overall Score Interpretation

Your score, at the 74th percentile, reflects a solid average score as compared to the norm (comparison) group indicated above. Compared with peers from this group, you display a good level of flexibility, skills, and motivation. Your capacity to apply agile behavior in learning situations is consistent, and with just a bit more focus, you can further enhance your agility and adaptability.

Subscale Scores

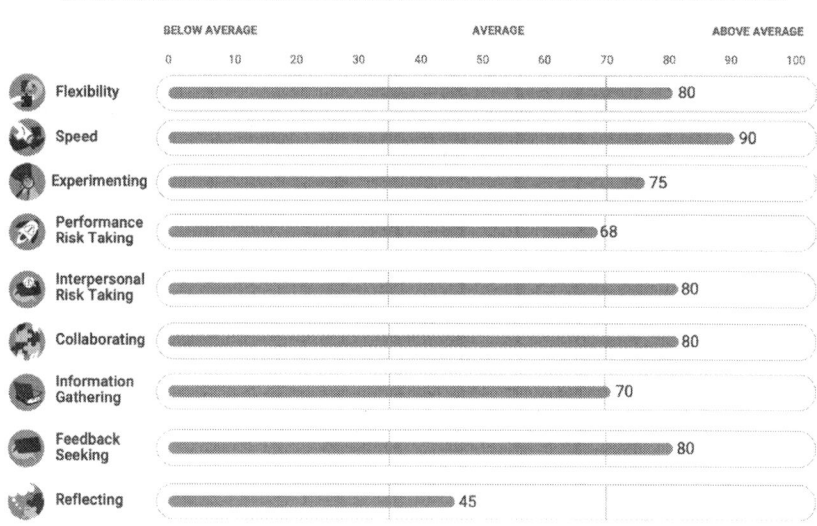

	BELOW AVERAGE	AVERAGE	ABOVE AVERAGE

0   10   20   30   40   50   60   70   80   90   100

Subscale	Score
Flexibility	80
Speed	90
Experimenting	75
Performance Risk Taking	68
Interpersonal Risk Taking	80
Collaborating	80
Information Gathering	70
Feedback Seeking	80
Reflecting	45

The group that does not seem to fit the results for the overall organization is sales and marketing. If we had acted only on the overall organizational results, we would have missed things that are unique to this function. *Speed* is much higher in sales and marketing. This makes sense, as these groups must react quickly to opportunities. This also aligns with a higher score in *Flexibility*, as sales and marketing must keep up with market changes and react quickly to them. We also see a lot more *Collaborating* in this composite. Once a team in a field office notices a new trend or change, they share it nationally among the sales force.

Sales and marketing people tend to be more extroverted, and it's not surprising to see more Interpersonal and *Performance Risk Taking* in this composite. However, *Reflecting* is something that is a little lower in this group than for the overall organization. Because sales and marketing tends to be more action oriented, its employees can be reluctant to slow down and review their performance.

Staff Composite Overall Scores
n = 75

Note: The percentile score by dimension represent the average
of all the respondents scores described as a percentage for each dimension.

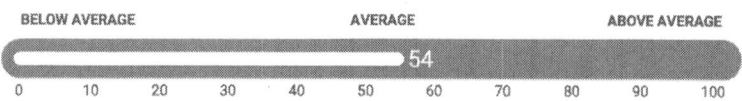

BELOW AVERAGE	AVERAGE	ABOVE AVERAGE

54

0   10   20   30   40   50   60   70   80   90   100

Overall Score Interpretation

Your score, at the 54th percentile, reflects a solid average score as compared to the norm (comparison) group indicated above. Compared with peers from this group, you display a good level of flexibility, skills, and motivation. Your capacity to apply agile behavior in learning situations is consistent, and with just a bit more focus, you can further enhance your agility and adaptability.

Subscale Scores

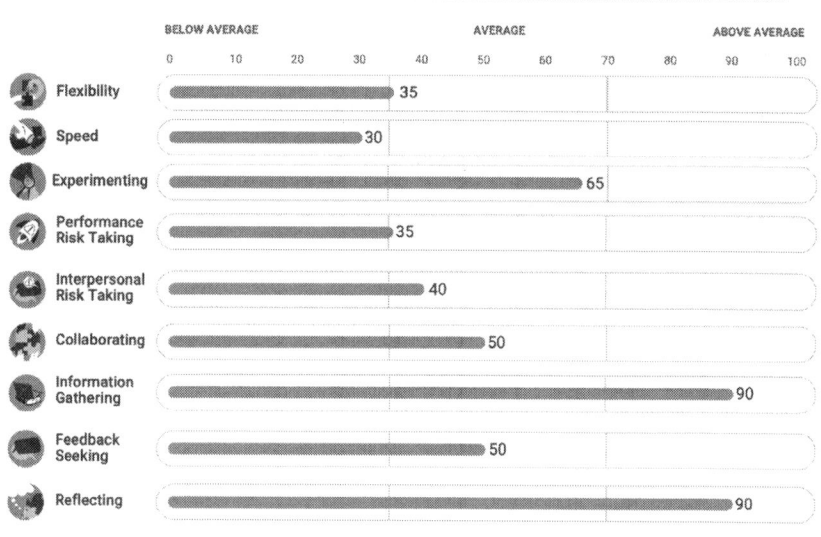

	BELOW AVERAGE	AVERAGE	ABOVE AVERAGE
Flexibility	35		
Speed	30		
Experimenting		65	
Performance Risk Taking	35		
Interpersonal Risk Taking	40		
Collaborating		50	
Information Gathering			90
Feedback Seeking		50	
Reflecting			90

We can see in this chart that *Flexibility* is a little lower with the staff group than in the overall organization. Employees in the staff group have been described by their line counterparts as territorial and frequently saying, "This is how we do things here." *Speed* and *Performance Risk Taking* also are a little lower for this group than the overall organization. This area of the company typically puts more emphasis on following policies than innovation. A place like Performax will need to clearly give people permission to take risks or make *Performance Risk Taking* a priority for it to start happening with the staff group.

Feedback Seeking is a little lower for staff than the overall organization. We find that in general, employees in the staff group at Performax are not seen by their peers as innovative. Some people speculate that employees in HR, finance and other departments don't want to draw attention to themselves by being innovative or to be held accountable by their internal customers.

We are not surprised that *Reflecting* is higher in the staff composite than the overall composite, as the functions in this group are notorious for analysis-paralysis, unless someone in senior management is asking the right questions and setting expectations.

IN SUMMARY

Reviewing these three sub-group composites with the organizational composite helps us identify three to five issues and ideas to improve learning agility dimensions for the organization overall and for the operations, sales and marketing, and staff functions. In response to the information we presented, the organization creates a cross-sectional task force that includes people from each of the functional groups and levels in the organization. The president's son offers to lead the task force and gives the group its first charge: using *Information Gathering*, one of its strengths, to drive change.

A smaller team within the task force agrees to summarize the data that's been collected and identify the top five opportunities for productivity improvement. This list will be narrowed to three by the senior management team. Each opportunity will become a project with specified goals, and each project will be seeded with two high-potential employees. These individuals will be told that the tasks they are assigned are designed to help them strengthen a personal learning agility dimension.

The dimensions of **Reflecting** and **Performance Risk Taking** will be combined and addressed by a second team. Since the staff group's composite *Burke Learning Agility Self-Assessment* percentile was high in this area, the team will be led by a person from human resources who has proven skills as a facilitator. This group will be given the mission to identity four projects: one each that will have the biggest performance impact for operations, sales and marketing, and staff groups, as well as the overall organization.

Each task force team will need to use a combination of the data gathered by the **Information Gathering** group. The projects will be designed to require **Reflecting** and **Performance Risk Taking** for Performax. In addition, two of the four projects will need to demonstrate **Collaborating**, and should involve high-potential employees from the operations and staff groups who need to strengthen these dimensions. Two of the groups, operations and staff, will need to focus on projects that demonstrate **Flexibility** for Performax and allow new ideas to be implemented. Updates from the task force will be presented monthly at each senior managers' staff meeting, and will be the first item on every agenda.

EPILOGUE

EPILOGUE: THE FUTURE BELONGS TO THE LEARNING AGILE

The future will not be built by perfect people. It will be shaped by courageous leaders and resilient professionals—those who are willing to learn continuously, flexibly, and faster than ever before. The architects of tomorrow will be those who understand that *learning agility* is not just a skill; it's a life force that transforms individuals, organizations, and entire societies.

As you, your team, your organization, and your community face accelerating demands to be future-ready and ambidextrous, learning agility becomes the single most critical capability for success. Being future-ready isn't about predicting flying cars or uploading your consciousness to the cloud. It's not about having all the answers. It's about developing the ability—at every level—to transform quickly and thrive, whether you anticipate change or are blindsided by it. Ambidextrous leadership means delivering high performance today while simultaneously building the capabilities needed for tomorrow.

WHAT'S NEXT?

Together with international partners, we have founded **Burke Assessments,** a company dedicated to extending the legacy of learning agility around the world. Through Burke Assessments, we are expanding research, collaborating globally, and continuously enriching the science behind learning agility.

We are partnering with universities worldwide to embed learning agility into the fabric of higher education. In a world of constant change, rising demands, and deep uncertainty, anxiety has become a defining challenge for students. By building learning agility into their educational journey, we aim to empower students to strengthen their confidence, resilience, and belief in their ability to navigate whatever lies ahead.

We hope this book has made a compelling case for why learning agility matters more than ever. Our deepest intention was to offer you more than a definition—to ignite in you a lasting commitment to develop and apply learning agility in your daily life.

As you close these pages, remember one vital truth:

- Learning agility is developable.
  Unlike personality, which tends to be more stable, learning agility is a set of behaviors you can cultivate through practice, feedback, and real-world experience.

  No matter where you start, the most important thing is this: *never stop learning*. Never stop stretching, reaching, experimenting, and growing.

  Join us.

  Follow our blog and LinkedIn page.

  Explore how learning agility can empower you—and those around you—to become your very best.

  The future will belong to those who can adapt, transform, and lead with courage.

  Let's build it together.

REFERENCES

Ames, C., & Archer, J. (1988). Achievement goals in the classroom: Students' learning strategies and motivation process. *Journal of Educational Psychology, 80*(3).

Bennis, W. G., & Thomas, R. J. (2007). *Leading for a lifetime: How defining moments shape the leaders of today and tomorrow.* Boston, MA: Harvard Business School Press.

Boyatzis, R. E. (1982). *The competent manager: A model for effective performance.* New York: Wiley & Sons, Inc.

Burke, W. (2016). *Burke learning agility inventory technical report.* St. Louis, MO: EASI•Consult®.

Collins, J. (2001). *Good to great.* New York: Harper Collins.

DeRue, D. S., Ashford, S. J., & Myers, C. G. (2012). Learning agility: In search of conceptual clarity and theoretical grounding. *Industrial and Organizational Psychology: Perspectives on Science and Practice, 5*(3), 258-279.

Dweck, C. S. (1986). Motivational processes affecting learning. *American Psychologist, 41,* 1040-1048.

Dweck, C. S. (2006). *Mindset.* New York: Ballantine Books.

Eichinger, R. W., & Lombardo, M. M. (2004). Learning agility as a prime indicator of potential. *Human Resource Planning, 27*(4), 12.

Goodwin, D. (2012). *Team of rivals.* New York: Simon and Schuster.

Hogan, R., Curphy, G. J., & Hogan, J. (1994). What we know about leadership: Effectiveness and personality. *American Psychologist, 49*(6), 493.

Hogan, J., Hogan, R., & Kaiser, R. B. (2009). Management derailment: Personality assessment and mitigation. In S. zedeck (Ed.), *American Psychological Association handbook of industrial and organizational psychology* (pp. 555-575). Washington, DC: American Psychological Association.

Kroll, M. D. (1988). Motivational orientations, views about the purpose of education, and intellectual styles. *Psychology in the Schools, 25,* 338-343.

Lewin, Kurt (1936). *Principles of topological psychology.* New York: McGrawHill.

Lombardo, M. M., & Eichinger, R. W. (2000). High potentials as high learners. *Human Resource Management, 39*(4), 321-329.

Lombardo, M. M., & Eichinger, R. W. (2007). *The leadership machine.* Minneapolis, Minn.

McCall, M. W. (2010). Recasting leadership development. *Industrial and Organizational Psychology, 3*(1), 3-19.

McCullough, D. (2015). *The Wright brothers.* New York: Simon and Schuster.

Morrison, R. F., & Brantner, T. M. (1992). What enhances or inhibits learning a new job? A basic career issue. *Journal of Applied Psychology, 77*(6), 926.

Moton, M. (2014). *Presidents and their generals.* Boston: Harvard University Press.

Pulakos, E. D., Arad, S., Donovan, M. A., & Plamondon, K. E. (2000). Adaptability in the workplace: Development of a taxonomy of adaptive performance. *Journal of Applied Psychology, 85*(4), 612-624.

Senge, P. M. (1990). *The fifth discipline: The art and practice of the learning organization.* New York: Doubleday/Currency.

Spreitzer, G. M., McCall, M. W., & Mahoney, J. D. (1997). Early identification of international executive potential. *Journal of Applied Psychology, 82*, 6–29.

Yu, M., Shan, J., Boutalikakas, A., Tempel, L., Balian, Z. (2022). What makes a company "future ready?". *Harvard Business Review.*

ABOUT THE AUTHORS

DAVID F. HOFF

David Hoff is the Founder and CEO of Burke Assessments. Previously he was Chief Operating Officer and Executive Vice President of Leadership and Development at EASI•Consult, a position he has held since 2003. David led organization transformation projects utilizing assessment and development expertise. David spent 17 years at Anheuser- Busch Companies, Inc. as Director of International Human Resources, Director of Human Resource Development and Selection, Manager of Management Development and Training and Organization Development Consultant. He's held corporate positions such as vice President of Human Resources for Dimension Data, Inc. and Managing Director of International Human Resources for Proxicom, Inc. In addition to a deep background in management and organization development, David has 10 years of international experience in Asia, Latin America and Europe. David has over 25 years of experience in the identification and application of competencies, starting in the late 70's working with David McClelland at McBer and Company. He did his graduate work at Teachers College, Columbia University earning an M.A. and M.Ed. He lives in Wilmington, N.C. with his wife Susan.

W. WARNER BURKE

W. Warner Burke is Professor Emeritus since 2022 at Teachers College, Columbia University where he was Professor of Psychology since 1979. Dr. Burke has authored or edited 20 books and written over 150 articles and book chapters. He has served as Editor of Organizational Dynamics, Academy of Management Executive, and the Journal of Applied Behavioral Science. He is a Fellow of the Academy of Management, Association of Psychological Science, the Society of Industrial and Organizational Psychology, and a Diplomate in industrial and organizational psychology, American Board of Professional Psychology. He has received several lifetime achievement awards, NASA's Public Service Medal, and The Outstanding Civilian Service Award from the Department of the Army.

Made in the USA
Middletown, DE
07 December 2025

21864856R00128